"PragerU has totally disrupted the university model, thank God!"

—Lord Andrew Roberts, author of *Churchill: Walking with Destiny*

"PragerU has brought higher education to the people at far less cost, with far more common sense, and with an agenda to offer critical knowledge without indoctrination."

—Victor Davis Hanson, senior fellow at the Hoover Institution at Stanford University and author of *The Second World Wars*

"If you want to waste money, you can spend $100,000 getting a pointless degree. If you want to learn, go to PragerU."

—Charlie Kirk, founder and CEO of Turning Point USA and author of *The College Scam*

THE *Honest Book* OF *Presidents*

THE *Honest Book* OF *Presidents*

The Men Who Shaped America

Edited by Allen Estrin

BROADSIDE BOOKS

HarperCollins books may be purchased for educational, business, or sales promotional use. For information, please email the Special Markets Department at SPsales@harpercollins.com.

hc.com

Images on pages 1, 5, 9, 13, 17, 21, 25, 29, 33, 37, 43, 47, 51, 55, 61, 65, 69, 73, 77, 81, 87, 93, 99, 103, 107, 113, 119, 123, 127, 133, 137, 141, 145, 149, 153, 157, 161, 165, 171, 177, 183, 189, 193, 197, 201, 205, 211, 215, 221, 225, 229, 233, 237, 243, 247, 253, and 259 created with generative AI.

FIRST EDITION

Library of Congress Cataloging-in-Publication Data has been applied for.

ISBN 978-0-06-343027-3

25 26 27 28 29 LBC 7 6 5 4 3

Contents

Preface

What kind of book is this?

First, it's a collection of individual biographies of American presidents, forty-five of them—George Washington through Donald Trump.

Second, this book is also a biography of a single entity—the United States of America. That's because each of these presidents, from the revered to the reviled, was the most important American of his day. Every major issue of the time—war, slavery, economic boom or bust—passed through 1600 Pennsylvania Avenue. Truman was right, the buck stopped here.

The book is also both factual and contextual; that is, our authors, some of the most distinguished historians and thinkers in America, explain the chief executives in the context of the era in which they lived. That's why we call it *The Honest Book of Presidents*. Our authors don't whitewash the truth, but they also don't paint it all black, either.

Above all, they try to be fair.

For example, James Buchanan, the president before Lincoln and always at or near the bottom of any presidential ranking list, didn't think he was going to precipitate the Civil War when he lobbied (improperly) for the infamous *Dred Scott* decision. On the contrary, he sincerely believed that the decision would save the country from armed conflict. Why he believed this is beautifully articulated in Joseph Fornieri's essay on the fifteenth president.

This book is also engaging.

Every one of our presidents has a story. Yes, that means you, James Monroe, and you, John Tyler and even you, Chester Alan Arthur.

James Monroe was the last of the Founding Fathers and the least known and appreciated. But he was a hero in the Revolutionary War, a hero in the War of 1812, and was so popular as president that he won a second term almost without opposition.

John Tyler was the first vice president to become president when William Henry Harrison died after only thirty days in office (how that happened is another fascinating story). The way Tyler became president is not as cut-and-dried as you might think. There's nothing in the Constitution that says the vice president must fill out the president's full term. You could easily read it to mean he was a caretaker until a new election could be arranged. That's in fact how many in Congress read it. But John Tyler had a different take. He was the president now, had moved into the White House, and there was nothing Congress could do to get him out. After due deliberation, Congress recognized, if reluctantly, that he had a point. Thus, Tyler set the precedent for all future "accidental" presidents: if a president dies in office, the VP takes over the remaining time of his term.

Chester Alan Arthur loved being vice president. The consummate machine politician, he had no responsibility and could attend social events to his heart's content. Becoming president was the last thing he wanted. But that's what happened when James Garfield was assassinated. How Arthur grew into the office is one of the great presidential stories.

This book is also short. None of the biographical essays is over a thousand words. This is by design.

There are many excellent full-length biographies about each of the American presidents. Nothing would give us greater joy than if this series inspired you to read them. I can promise that you will be richly rewarded for the effort. But the fact is, few people, relatively speaking, are going to read a thousand-page biography of Ulysses Grant or Harry Truman, let alone Millard Fillmore or Benjamin Harrison.

It's much more likely that they will read a short essay (or watch the corresponding five-minute video on our website PragerU.com) about these men.

Given the sad state of American public education, the general knowledge of our presidents is not great, to put it mildly. Come on, how much do you really know about Zachary Taylor? (How about this tidbit: had he lived out his term, he might have found a way to prevent the Civil War.) And what do you know about Warren Harding? That will improve exponentially once you read Amity Shlaes's essay about him. Not only that, you'll be impressed by how effective a president he really was. He was followed by an even better one.

A few presidents get the two-essay treatment. Too much happened during the terms of George Washington, Abraham Lincoln, Teddy Roosevelt, Woodrow Wilson, Franklin Roosevelt, Harry Truman, Dwight Eisenhower, John Kennedy, and Lyndon Johnson to squeeze into a single essay. This is also the case with our more recent presidents—Bill Clinton, George W. Bush, and Barack Obama—whose terms most of us actually lived through and are therefore naturally more familiar.

How much can you learn in the short amount of time it will take you to read (or watch) these presidential biographies?

A lot.

We have a treasure trove of anecdotal evidence—comments and emails we've received—that this is true. We also have data. The PragerU presidential videos have been seen by tens of millions of people.

In addition to educating yourself, the series is a great way to educate your family about the presidents and American history. These videos are appropriate for young people grade nine and above. Before, say, dinner, ask them to read the essay. Then, as a family, watch the

PragerU video. This will take about fifteen minutes. During the meal, discuss the president and what you all learned about him. Work your way (at your own pace) through the entire series. Voilà, you have just homeschooled your children. And yourself.

What kind of book is this?

One that's full of surprises, American style.

Turn the page and find out.

Allen Estrin
Co-founder and Executive Director, PragerU
Sherman Oaks, California

THE *Honest Book* OF *Presidents*

CHAPTER 1

WHAT MADE GEORGE WASHINGTON GREAT?

By John Rhodehamel

It's hard to imagine there would have been a United States of America without George Washington.

He was there at the birth of the nation. He successfully guided it through war and nurtured it in peace.

How did he do it?

Not by being a great general, a potent political theorist, or even a clever politician. He was none of those things.

And yet, he was admired by generals, political theorists, and politicians. Why?

Because he was a man great men trusted. Thomas Jefferson, John Adams, Benjamin Franklin, James Madison, and so many others looked up to him—literally. He was one of the tallest men of his era at six feet three. Add courage, integrity, and wisdom, and you have a truly impressive figure.

Let's start with his courage. That was never in doubt. If anything, he had too much of it.

Bold to the point of rashness as a young man, he fought for the British against the French over control of the Ohio Valley, then the westernmost point of the American wilderness.

Throughout that conflict, known as the French and Indian War, and the American Revolution, Washington was always in the thick of the action. His aides often struggled to keep him from surging too far ahead of his own troops. In one battle, his coat was pierced four times by musket fire. Horses were shot out from under him. Amazingly, some would say miraculously, he was never wounded—not so much as a flesh wound.

By the time the revolution broke out in April 1775, Washington was firmly committed to the cause of American independence. He arrived in Philadelphia in May of that year to offer his services to the Continental Congress. He was quickly made commander of the new rebel army. There was only one problem: there was no army to speak of. There was just a ragtag collection of state militias. How was Washington going to defeat the greatest military force in the world with that?

It was a problem the general struggled with for eight and a half years. That he managed to hold the army together, organize it into a disciplined fighting force, and guide it to victory was testament to his fortitude, his patience, and his personal bravery.

Of his integrity, one need only to look at what he did when the war ended: exactly what he promised to do when the war began. He resigned his military command and went home to Mount Vernon.

By stepping down, Washington raised himself up as the embodiment of republican heroism. It is said that King George III asked the London-based American painter Benjamin West what Washington was likely to do when peace came. West replied that Washington would probably return to his farm. The king was astounded. "If he does that," His Majesty declared, "he will be the greatest man in the world!"

This story may be apocryphal, but the Newburgh Rebellion, and how Washington handled it, is not. With experience had come wisdom.

As the revolution wound down, a group of officers refused to give up their arms until they were paid. If they didn't get their money, which Congress didn't have, they would take control of the government. It was not an idle threat. No less a figure than Alexander Hamilton was in a panic.

Washington, no great orator, sought to defuse their anger. They had risked everything to create a republican society, he told the officers. To abandon the cause now, when true victory was so close, would mean all their sacrifices would have been in vain.

However convincing the speech may have been, it was a simple gesture that carried the day. Washington concluded his remarks by reading to them a letter sent to him from a member of Congress. Suddenly, he stopped. From his pocket, he pulled a pair of spectacles. None of the officers had ever seen him wear them. Putting the glasses on, Washington said, "Gentlemen, you must pardon me. I have grown gray in the service of my country and now find myself going blind."

He finished reading the letter and left the hall without another word. The gesture, sincerely offered with just the right touch of stagecraft, pierced the hearts of his men. Many were moved to tears. They immediately passed a resolution declaring their loyalty to civilian government. George Washington had saved the revolution once again.

It wouldn't be the last time. During the writing of the Constitution and during his eight years as president, Washington was repeatedly called upon to hold the fractious young nation together. He never failed to do so.

We commonly refer to George Washington now as the father of our country. It's hard to imagine any nation ever had a better one.

John Rhodehamel is the former archivist of the Washington Library at Mount Vernon, Virginia, and curator of American historical manuscripts at the Huntington Library in San Marino, California. He is a leading authority on America's two most iconic presidents—George Washington and Abraham Lincoln—having written *George Washington: The Wonder of the Age*, *The Great Experiment: George Washington and the American Republic*, *The Last Best Hope of Earth: Abraham Lincoln and the Promise of America*, and *America's Original Sin: White Supremacy, John Wilkes Booth, and the Lincoln Assassination*.

In addition, he has edited several books, including *The American Revolution: Writings from the War of Independence*, *George Washington: Writings*, *Letters of Liberty: A Documentary History of the U.S. Constitution*, and *Right or Wrong, God Judge Me: The Writings of John Wilkes Booth*.

CHAPTER 2

GEORGE WASHINGTON

A General Without an Army

By Edward Lengel

When the American colonies went to war in 1775 against Great Britain, the greatest military power on earth, they did it without an army.

There were local militias here and there, but no army in any organized sense.

But . . . the Americans did have a general.

His name, of course, was George Washington.

What possessed this man, a prosperous Virginia farmer, to take on such a dangerous, seemingly hopeless mission?

Washington fervently believed in the cause of independence.

He was willing to risk everything to make this ambition a reality.

And he believed there was a chance America could win.

He believed it because, ironically, he had fought for the British. He knew their strengths—certainly—but he also knew their weaknesses.

Washington's "education" began in 1753 at the tender age of twenty-one.

Ambitious for a military life, Washington volunteered to deliver an ultimatum from the royal governor of Virginia to the commander of the French forces in the Ohio River Valley. The ultimatum said this to the French: This is our colonial territory not yours. Vacate or face the consequences.

Although military command was completely new to him, Washington already displayed the intangibles of leadership: decisiveness, the ability to stay calm under pressure, and physical courage. What he lacked in sound judgment—he was twenty-one—he made up for in sheer determination. He endured extreme hardships without complaint, facing near-death experiences without flinching. Almost freezing to death and nearly drowning in an icy river were only two examples. That the French commander scoffed at the Virginia governor's demands was disappointing, but that wasn't Washington's fault.

The following year, 1754, Washington was appointed lieutenant colonel of the Virginia Regiment and was once again sent to the frontier to engage the French.

When Washington, near what is now Pittsburgh, became convinced that the French were preparing to ambush him, he decided to make a preemptive attack.

In the ensuing battle a French officer, Ensign Jumonville, and nine of his men were killed.

The French didn't take it well. They sent a force to track Washington down. Washington decided to make his stand at a small, hastily built enclosure he dubbed Fort Necessity. It should have been his last stand. In a driving rain, the French surrounded the fort and opened fire. One hundred of Washington's men were either killed or wounded before he finally surrendered. The terms of surrender were written, of course, in French, which Washington didn't understand. To his great dismay, he later learned that in signing the document he had admitted to ordering the "assassination" of Jumonville.

The French later used this "admission" to justify their claim that it was the British who started what became known as the Seven Years' War in Europe, or the French and Indian War in the colonies. In the words of English writer and politician Sir Horace Walpole, "The volley fired by a young Virginian in the backwoods of America set the world on fire."

This was the first time Washington's name was heard in the courts of Europe. It would not, of course, be the last.

In 1755, Washington was attached to British forces led by General Edward Braddock. The British were determined to drive the French out of North America. Washington supported this ambition but was appalled by the execution.

Braddock's plan failed to account for the fighting prowess of the French and especially the Indians and especially in dense forest wilderness. When the French and Indians attacked in what became known as the Battle of the Monongahela, the British literally didn't know what hit them. The enemy seemed to be firing from behind every tree. The bloodshed was appalling. Braddock paid the ultimate price. He was killed, along with 456 of his men.

Washington, who had two horses shot out from under him and had four bullets pierce his clothes and hat, took charge of the remnants of the British army. His ability to stay cool under fire became the stuff of instant legend.

Washington was now a combat veteran. The Braddock disaster seared into his mind the gravity of war. He would forever carry this with him. It shaped his military strategy. He would never sacrifice his men needlessly.

He also learned that there is no substitute for discipline. It's a myth that Washington was a fan of sharpshooting backwoodsmen. Just the opposite. Instilling discipline, to Washington, was his first job as a leader. Fighting effectiveness, he believed, depended on that.

Twenty years after the Battle of Monongahela, John Adams stepped forward in Congress to recommend a commander for the Continental army that didn't yet exist. To Adams and many others, Washington, now forty-three years old, married, and a leading citizen of Virginia, was an obvious choice.

Adams was doing Washington no favors.

But Adams was right.

There was only one man for the job.

Edward Lengel received his Ph.D. from the University of Virginia, where he was a professor and directed the Washington Papers Project for many years. He has held several high-profile positions, such as executive director of the Texas Historical Commission, chief historian of the White House Historical Association, senior director of programs at the National WWII Museum, and chief historian at the National Medal of Honor Museum.

Also a professional author, speaker, and battlefield tour guide, Lengel has written fourteen books on American history, including *General George Washington: A Military Life*; *Inventing George Washington: America's Founder, in Myth & Memory*; and *First Entrepreneur: How George Washington Built His—and the Nation's—Prosperity.*

Lengel is a corecipient of the National Humanities Medal. He has made frequent television and radio appearances on the History Channel, FOX News, SiriusXM, and National Public Radio.

CHAPTER 3

JOHN ADAMS

American Founder and Second President

By C. Bradley Thompson

Everybody knows what happened on July 4, 1776: America was born. But three days earlier, on July 1, independence hung in the balance.

There was a great case to be made not to secede from Great Britain. The colonists had no army, no navy, and almost no money. England had a lot of all three. It would have made perfect sense to bend to the will of the Crown, pay some extra taxes, and call it a day. There were plenty of people in Philadelphia prepared to make that case. They could have easily prevailed. Yet they didn't. They didn't because of the words of one man: John Adams.

At a key moment in the congressional debate, when the forces against independence appeared to have the upper hand, Adams rose to his feet. Without notes and without any preparation, he made the case for independence. By the time he sat down, the case had been won. We don't have a transcript of what he said. If we did, Adams might rank even higher than he does now among the Founding Fathers. Thomas Jefferson said years later that the speech was so powerful in "thought and expression" that it "moved us from our seats." Adams was, Jefferson said, "our Colossus on the floor."

If Washington was the sword of the American Revolution, and Jefferson the pen, then Adams was its engine. Brilliant, demanding, meticulous, but often irascible, he was not an easy man to love. At some point in his life, he irritated, if not alienated, everyone with whom he worked. Yet these same people would invariably come to appreciate him. That included Washington and especially Jefferson, with whom he sometimes fought bitterly.

Ironically, for all his cantankerousness, his marriage to Abigail Adams stands as one of the great love stories of American history. Their correspondence, spanning five decades, is a vibrant, living history of the nation's early years. Abigail frankly described her husband as "short, thick, and fat." But what he lacked in good looks and physical stature he made up for in intellect, personal integrity, and clarity of thought.

Born in 1735 near Boston, Adams relentlessly pushed himself to rise early, work hard, and live a moral life. He strove—in the language of the day—for a life of virtue over vice. He first came to public attention in 1765, when he issued a stirring rebuke of the much-hated Stamp Act. For the next eighteen years, he fought unceasingly against British tyranny and for American liberty, dedicating his life, his fortune, and his sacred honor to the struggle.

These were not idle words. In his forties by the time of the revolution, he didn't fight in the war; instead, he crossed the Atlantic four times on diplomatic missions, braving winter storms, diseases such as pneumonia and dysentery, and British warships. Capture would have meant summary execution.

In Europe, as befit his character, he was all business. He helped Benjamin Franklin bring the French into the war on the American side, and he arranged critical loans from Dutch banks. When the war ended, it was Adams, along with Franklin and John Jay, who negotiated the treaty in which England officially recognized the new United States.

For all these efforts, Adams was paid virtually nothing. But fortune was never his aim. Creating a new, better, freer country than the world had ever known was all that he cared about. As one delegate to the Continental Congress said, "The man to whom the country is most indebted for the great measure of independence is Mr. John Adams."

Following the war, Adams served two terms as vice president under George Washington and then one term as the second president of the United States. Taking over for Washington was a thankless task. Everyone deferred to the great general. To put it mildly, Adams was not granted the same courtesy. Still, the new president was able to distinguish his time in high office with two significant achievements: one marked by something he did do; the other, by something he did not do.

What he did was convince the Congress to build a navy. Given the strong opposition to any kind of standing military, this was no mean feat. But Adams was adamant that the United States could not become a great nation without a great navy. He pushed through the legislation that made it possible.

What he did not do was get the country involved in the war in Europe. France insisted that America join it in its fight against England. France had come to America's aid during the fight for independence, the French argued. Here was America's chance to repay the debt. Adams firmly declined. The infant nation was in no position to wage war for or against anyone.

As the fiftieth anniversary of the Declaration of Independence approached, a ninety-one-year-old Adams was asked to provide a toast for the upcoming celebration. He offered two words: "independence forever." It turned out to be his last public utterance.

How fitting.

C. Bradley Thompson is a professor of political science at Clemson University, where he teaches political philosophy. He is also the executive director of the Clemson Institute for the Study of Capitalism, the founder of the Lyceum Scholars Program, and author of *America's Revolutionary Mind: A Moral History of the American Revolution and the Declaration That Defined It.*

During his academic career, he has been the Garwood Family Professor in the James Madison Program at Princeton University, a John Adams Fellow at the Institute of United States Studies (University of London), and a Fellow of the Program in Constitutional Studies at Harvard University.

His first book, *John Adams and the Spirit of Liberty*, was awarded the Best First Book in Political Theory prize in 1999 by the American Political Science Association.

CHAPTER 4

THE GENIUS OF THOMAS JEFFERSON

By Carol Swain

There's a reason why Thomas Jefferson's face is on our coinage; why his sculpted head is on Mount Rushmore; and why there is a magnificent memorial in his honor in Washington, DC.

As British historian Paul Johnson put it in *A History of the American People*, "no one did more than [Jefferson] did to create the United States of America."

Born on April 13, 1743, in Shadwell, Virginia, Jefferson early on displayed an intellectual curiosity that would never be quenched.

He devoured books on history, science, math, and philosophy, while learning Latin, Greek, and French. He would eventually amass a personal library of sixty-five hundred volumes, declaring, "I cannot live without books."

There was virtually no subject that he didn't find fascinating and didn't try to master. Most of the time, he succeeded.

He graduated from college in just two years with a plan to practice law. At age twenty-five, he won a seat in Virginia's House of Burgesses—Virginia's colonial equivalent of a House of Representatives—entering politics just as the American colonies were beginning to challenge British rule.

Although Jefferson was not a gifted speaker, he was a genius with words.

This gift did not go unnoticed.

John Adams and Benjamin Franklin—no rhetorical slouches themselves—asked him to write the first draft of America's Declaration of Independence.

Their confidence was richly rewarded. Jefferson's assertions that "all men are created equal," and that "nature's God . . . their Creator" had granted them "inalienable" rights formed the cornerstones of the American experiment.

Jefferson was not yet thirty-four.

In 1790, President Washington appointed him to be the new nation's first secretary of state, one of the two key posts in Washington's cabinet. The other post was secretary of the treasury, to which Washington appointed Alexander Hamilton.

The two became bitter rivals. Jefferson distrusted Hamilton's belief in a powerful central government; Hamilton thought Jefferson was an impractical dreamer.

Both misunderstood the other. This was probably inevitable, given their strong convictions and considerable egos. And although it's true that Jefferson was a lofty political theorist, he was also a cunning politician.

His hardball tactics angered or alienated people who had once been close allies—most notably John Adams.

After defeating Adams in a contentious election in 1800, Jefferson served two terms as America's third president—a tenure historians still consider among the most consequential and successful in American history.

He reduced the scope and reach of the federal government—cutting taxes, lowering spending, and retiring half of the national debt.

This was the small-government Jefferson in action. But he had no problem exercising vigorous executive authority when he felt it was necessary. Nowhere is this better expressed than his greatest accomplishment as president: the acquisition of the Louisiana Territory from France for $15 million, or just 4 cents an acre.

In one fell swoop, Jefferson orchestrated a deal that doubled the size of the United States, incorporating territories of what are now fifteen states, while also eliminating the presence of a powerful European empire from North America.

After completing two terms, Jefferson, following Washington's example, stepped down from the first office.

He spent the last seventeen years of his life at his beloved home, Monticello, an estate he built not far from his birthplace.

There, he not only founded the University of Virginia, but repaired his relationship with his long-lost friend John Adams. They began a fabled correspondence that continued nearly to the end of their lives.

Remarkably—if one is so inclined, one may even say providentially—Jefferson and Adams died on the same day, July 4, 1826, the fiftieth anniversary of the signing of Jefferson's Declaration of Independence.

Thomas Jefferson was a complex man who must be judged in the context of his time. This is, of course, best understood in his relationship to slavery. He grew up in a world that took slave ownership for granted. He owned slaves as his father had before him. Yet he abhorred the very idea of slavery. On numerous occasions, he acknowledged that he violated his fundamental belief that "all men are created equal."

And yet it is also true that Jefferson pointed the way out of that heinous institution. For this we are forever in his debt.

Abraham Lincoln knew this. Of the Declaration of Independence, Lincoln wrote: "[Thomas Jefferson gave] liberty, not alone to the people of this country, but hope to the world for all future time."

Born into abject poverty in rural Virginia, Carol Swain earned five degrees and obtained early tenure at Princeton and full professorship at Vanderbilt, where she was professor of political science and a professor of law. Today she is a sought-after cable news contributor, prominent national speaker, and bestselling author.

In addition to three presidential appointments, Swain is a former Distinguished Senior Fellow for Constitutional Studies with the Texas Public Policy Foundation, having also served on the Tennessee Advisory Committee to the US Civil Rights Commission, the National Endowment for the Humanities, and the 1776 Commission.

An award-winning political scientist, cited three times by the US Supreme Court, she has authored or edited eleven published books and numerous opinion pieces for major national publications. Her television appearances include BBC Radio and TV, C-SPAN, ABC News, CNN, and FOX News.

CHAPTER 5

JAMES MADISON

The Great Pragmatist

By Jay Cost

From the time he joined the Continental Congress in 1780 through his second term as the fourth president of the United States, James Madison was in the middle of . . . everything.

When it came to the Constitution, he understood it better than any single person—because nobody contributed more to its creation.

When it came to selling that document to the American people, he made the most persuasive arguments.

When ten amendments—the Bill of Rights—were needed to seal the deal, he wrote those, too.

Diminutive in stature—he was just over five feet tall—he was a giant in every other respect: as a writer, theorist, and, most importantly, political pragmatist. He was a deep thinker who got things done. And no one ever worked harder to get those things done.

James Madison was born in 1751 to a prosperous family in the Virginia Piedmont. Like his mentor, neighbor, and best friend, Thomas Jefferson, he was well educated in the classics and spoke multiple languages. His home state sent him as a delegate to the Continental Congress in 1780, at the age of twenty-nine. There, he saw firsthand how bad a national government could be: slow, corrupt, self-interested.

He resolved to do something about it.

He wasn't alone. George Washington and others pushed for a new social compact, a document that would truly bind the divergent interests of the various states—no easy feat. Their efforts paid off in May 1787 when a new Constitutional Convention was convened in Philadelphia.

Even though he was one of the younger delegates, Madison took a lead role, not because he was so ambitious, but because he was so knowledgeable. He attended every session, gave more speeches than anyone, took meticulous notes, and drafted the plan that the delegates used as the framework for the new Constitution.

Writing the document was hard enough; selling it to the American people would prove even harder. A group known as the Anti-Federalists began flooding the newspapers with anti-Constitution essays, warning that the plan would destroy liberty rather than save it.

Madison and New York lawyer Alexander Hamilton came to the Constitution's defense in a series of essays known as the Federalist Papers. The two men were a dynamic duo. Hamilton did the lion's share of the writing, but Madison's submissions arguably had the most impact. He carefully explained the system of checks and balances that would define the new government.

The Federalists carried the day—just barely—and the Constitution was ratified.

Madison wasn't yet forty. . . . And still a bachelor.

That changed when he met Dolley Payne, a lively young widow seventeen years his junior. She transformed the solitary, workaholic Madison into one of the great dinner party hosts of the era. This proved invaluable to his political career.

After serving as Thomas Jefferson's secretary of state and supervising the purchase of the Louisiana Territory from the French, doubling the size of the United States, Madison was the obvious choice to become the fourth president.

But there was trouble on the horizon. Great Britain, which had never fully reconciled itself to its defeat in the Revolutionary War, continued to harass the new nation at every turn. It seized American goods at sea and even forced American sailors to work for the Royal Navy.

By June 1812, Madison had had enough. He asked Congress to declare war against Great Britain for continued abuses of American rights. So began the War of 1812.

It was a disaster—one of the rare times Madison failed to think through an important policy decision. The United States simply wasn't prepared for war, certainly not one against the mightiest power on earth.

At the low point in the conflict, Madison had to flee the White House or risk capture. In the chaos, Dolley famously saved the priceless Gilbert Stuart portrait of George Washington by having it ripped from its frame.

Eventually, American forces found their footing, winning three decisive victories—at Plattsburgh, Baltimore, and New Orleans. The two sides agreed to peace terms that essentially amounted to a draw.

But to the American people, it was a glorious victory, and Madison had guided them to it. The young nation had demonstrated once and for all that the United States could not be pushed around. The War of 1812 has rightly been remembered as America's second war for independence.

In the spring of 1817, Madison retired to Montpelier, his estate in the Virginia Piedmont, having dedicated roughly forty years to politics. When he started his career, the United States wasn't even a nation. When he finished, it was well on its way to becoming a world power. Many patriots contributed to the country's success, but few, if any, did as much as James Madison.

Jay Cost is the Gerald R. Ford Nonresident Senior Fellow at the American Enterprise Institute (AEI), where he focuses on political theory, Congress, and elections. He is also a Visiting Scholar at Grove City College. a contributing editor at the *Washington Examiner*, and a former writer for the political website RealClearPolitics.

His books include *Democracy or Republic? The People and the Constitution*; *James Madison: America's First Politician*; *The Price of Greatness: Alexander Hamilton, James Madison, and the Creation of American Oligarchy*; *Spoiled Rotten: How the Politics of Patronage Corrupted the Once Noble Democratic Party and Now Threatens the American Republic*; and *A Republic No More: Big Government and the Rise of Political Corruption*.

Cost has a Ph.D. and an M.A. in political science from the University of Chicago and a B.A. in government and history from the University of Virginia.

CHAPTER 6

JAMES MONROE

The Last Founding Father

By Chris DeRose

On December 26, 1776, eighteen-year-old James Monroe lay dying outside of Trenton, New Jersey. A musket ball had penetrated his left shoulder, severing a major artery.

The opening months of the Revolutionary War had been a disaster for the American side.

General George Washington desperately needed a victory. He launched a surprise attack against British mercenaries camped at Trenton.

Monroe led the vanguard to secure the roads in and out of town. If the fate of the revolution rested on the Battle of Trenton, the Battle of Trenton rested on Monroe's success.

Monroe accomplished his mission. Washington and the Americans had their victory. But it looked like it was going to cost Monroe his life.

Fortunately, a local doctor got to him and stopped the bleeding. That doctor saved the life of a man who went on to play a critical role in the first fifty years of the new American nation.

James Monroe had humbler beginnings than many of the other Founders. Both parents died by the time he was sixteen, leaving him responsible for four siblings and the family farm. He was able to attend the College of William and Mary only with help from an uncle. He didn't stay long, however, joining Washington's army at the outset of the revolution.

After his time in the army, Monroe returned to Virginia to study law but soon turned his attention to politics. He represented Virginia in the Continental Congress, where he met his wife, Elizabeth, the daughter of a prominent New York City merchant. They married after a short courtship. It was a genuine love match and one of the great romances of the founding era.

During this time, Monroe also developed a close friendship with fellow Virginian James Madison. But the friends found themselves on opposite sides of the critical issue of the day: the fate of the new Constitution.

In one of the least appreciated, but most important episodes in American history, Madison and Monroe ran against each other in the first congressional election in 1789. Monroe opposed the Constitution because it lacked a guarantee of fundamental rights, like freedom of speech and freedom of religion. Madison believed those rights were already secured by the limits on government in the Constitution.

Madison won the election, but Monroe won the argument. Madison recognized that a Bill of Rights would be needed in order for the Constitution to be broadly accepted by the people.

After serving terms as a senator and as governor of Virginia, Monroe was sent to France by President Thomas Jefferson to buy the city of New Orleans from the French emperor, Napoleon. But to Monroe's surprise, Napoleon offered Monroe not just New Orleans but the entire Louisiana Territory.

Monroe had a problem. He didn't have any authorization to make such a large purchase. He decided to make it anyway, doubling the size of the United States.

Had Monroe done nothing else, his place in American history would have been secured. But his greatest contributions were still ahead.

In the War of 1812, President Madison relied more on Monroe than anybody. Monroe served as both secretary of state and as acting secretary of war. Working tirelessly for days on end, often with little sleep, Monroe helped Madison stave off disaster and achieve a negotiated peace with Great Britain.

When Madison's second term ended, Monroe was the natural choice to replace him. He won the 1816 election decisively and became the fifth president of the United States.

Perhaps more than any Founder, Monroe had a vision for America as a growing, expanding nation. He negotiated with the British to demilitarize the Great Lakes, established much of our northern border, and set the stage for future American ownership of the Oregon Territory in the West. In the South, he acquired Florida from Spain in exchange for settling some outstanding claims. And he signed the Missouri Compromise, which diffused a major domestic crisis that threatened to split the nation. The compromise would draw a line across the country: new states above the line would be free states, and new states below the line would be slave states.

Instead of civil war, this time became known as the Era of Good Feelings. Monroe won reelection in 1820—unopposed.

His most enduring accomplishment would come in his second term: the doctrine that bears his name. The Monroe Doctrine declared that the United States would not permit European powers to colonize the Western Hemisphere. In doing so, he put the world on notice: the young nation was now a major power.

While Monroe did as much as any president to secure America's prosperous future, he had much less success securing his own.

He left the White House deeply in debt—most of it expenses he had incurred on the government's behalf.

Monroe was forced to sell almost everything he owned and live with his daughter in New York City. He died in 1831, and, like Adams and Jefferson before him, on the Fourth of July.

We're lucky he didn't perish on that roadside in Trenton.

Chris DeRose is the *New York Times* bestselling author of *The Fighting Bunch: The Battle of Athens and How World War II Veterans Won the Only Successful Armed Rebellion Since the Revolution*; *Star Spangled Scandal: Sex, Murder, and the Trial That Changed America*; *The Presidents' War: Six American Presidents and the Civil War That Divided Them*; *Congressman Lincoln: The Making of America's Greatest President*; and *Founding Rivals: Madison vs. Monroe, the Bill of Rights, and the Election That Saved a Nation.*

DeRose was formerly a law professor and senior litigation counsel to the Arizona attorney general, a professor of constitutional law, and clerk of the Superior Court for Maricopa County, leading a team of over seven hundred professionals in serving America's fourth-largest county.

CHAPTER 7

JOHN QUINCY ADAMS

Dedicated to America

By Jane Hampton Cook

Imagine your father expected you to grow up to be president of the United States.

Now imagine you did.

That was John Quincy Adams.

His father, John Adams, was a leading figure in the American Revolution and the second president of the United States.

That's a lot to live up to.

But John Quincy did it . . . and more.

Born on July 11, 1767, near Boston, he grew up in a time of turmoil. At the age of seven, in 1775, he watched the Battle of Bunker Hill from a hilltop near his family home.

In 1778, Congress sent his father to Paris to help convince the French to support the American War of Independence. John Quincy traveled with him—a ten-year-old diplomat in training.

And what a training it was.

For the next seven years, in addition to France, John Quincy lived in Great Britain, the Netherlands, Russia, and Sweden, learning firsthand the art of diplomacy.

By the time he returned to the United States in 1785 at the age of eighteen, he had absorbed not only the customs of these countries but learned to speak their languages as well.

After graduating from Harvard, he took up the law. But reading legal documents all day bored him to tears. The world was changing fast, and he wanted to be in the middle of it.

Which is right where he landed.

George Washington—who always had a keen eye for exceptionally talented young men—appointed him the American ambassador to the Netherlands. That subsequently led him to the court of Russian Czar Alexander I, and then to the court of British King George III.

He reached the peak of his diplomatic career in 1814, when he negotiated the end of the disastrous War of 1812, between Great Britain and the United States.

Although the British, as the stronger power, had the leverage, Adams and his colleagues held their ground. The final settlement, named the Treaty of Ghent after the Belgian city where it was signed, was essentially a wash for the British but a victory for the Americans, who, from their point of view, had defeated the British a second time.

Adams now stood alone as America's foremost diplomat.

When his friend James Monroe became president in 1817, he appointed Adams secretary of state. The two men forged a highly productive partnership.

Their most lasting accomplishment was the Monroe Doctrine, issued in 1823. The doctrine announced that America would not permit European colonization in the Western Hemisphere. Although the doctrine bears the name of the fifth president, it originated with his secretary of state. It remains a fundamental principle of American foreign policy.

Adams's many accomplishments made him the logical successor to Monroe.

But the hero of the War of 1812, Andrew Jackson, begged to differ. In the 1824 presidential election, Jackson ran against Adams.

Jackson won the popular vote but couldn't secure a majority in the Electoral College. This forced the decision as to who would be the next president into the House of Representatives.

When Henry Clay, the influential Speaker of the House, threw his support to Adams, the son of the second president became the sixth president.

Adams had achieved his ultimate goal.

It brought him nothing but misery.

His ambitious agenda—to build a national system of roads and canals, establish a national university, and expand foreign trade—got nowhere.

Jackson's allies in Congress—soon to call themselves Democrats—blocked him at every turn.

The presidency revealed Adams's weakness as a politician. Brilliant and forward-looking, he was a man for the people, but not a man of the people. In the 1828 election—a rematch with Jackson—Adams opted to remain above the fray. But that was the style of yesterday. This time the charismatic general won easily.

Adams left the White House a dejected figure, lamenting, "The Sun of my political life sets in the deepest gloom."

As it turned out, a new phase of his illustrious career was beginning.

Against his wife Louisa's advice—in fact, against the advice of practically everyone he knew—he ran for Congress in 1830.

For most people, this would have been a humiliating demotion, but for Adams it was a way to stay in the fight.

During his nine terms, Adams was Congress's most outspoken opponent of slavery, so outspoken in fact that his proslavery enemies tried to shut him up. Literally. They imposed the infamous "gag rule" in 1836 to prevent any discussion of the slavery issue on the House floor. But the Southern Democrats and their Northern allies proved no match for Adams, who repeatedly thwarted their designs. Nobody ever figured out a way to keep Adams silent for long.

Nobody, that is, except Father Time.

On February 21, 1848, Adams, now eighty, still at his post, still defending the right of all men to be free, collapsed in the House chamber. He died two days later.

John Quincy Adams was far from America's most successful president, but by his own high standard, his record of public service has never been equaled.

Jane Hampton Cook is an award-winning author of ten books, a national media commentator, columnist, a former White House communication staffer, and a presidential historian. She is the author of *Battlefields and Blessings*, *American Phoenix*, *The Burning of the White House*, *War of Lies*, *The Faith of America's First Ladies*, and *Resilience on Parade*.

Cook is a frequent guest on the FOX News Channel and WMAL, and has appeared on CNN, BBC, Sky News, and CNBC. An on-camera storyteller and cast member, she has appeared on Brian Kilmeade's *What Made America Great?*, the George Washington documentary *The First American*, and the History Channel's *United Stuff of America*.

CHAPTER 8

ANDREW JACKSON

The People's President

By Allen Guelzo

No American president has been more beloved and reviled than Andrew Jackson, the seventh president of the United States. This was as true during his own day as it is in ours.

Andrew Jackson was born in South Carolina on March 15, 1767. He was barely ten years old when the American Revolution broke out. The war claimed the lives of his two brothers and his mother, leaving Jackson orphaned, alone, and with a bitter hatred for all things British.

In time, he would get his revenge.

Tall, with sharp features topped by a thatch of red hair, Jackson always made an impression. In 1788, after a brief study of the law, he wangled an appointment as a district attorney in Tennessee, then known as the Southwest Territories, began investing in land and slaves, and earned an appointment as major general of the Tennessee militia. Though he had no formal military training, he was a natural leader. The men under his command would follow him anywhere. And if they didn't, he might hang them. He fought numerous duels. He killed a man, Charles Dickinson, in one. That was Jackson.

As Jackson's investments and military reputation advanced, so did his political interests. He served in Congress when Tennessee became a state in 1796 and later briefly as senator. His politics were decidedly Jeffersonian. He believed that owning land was the only real wealth; that industry, commerce, and banking were financial traps that ultimately benefited the rich at the expense of everyone else.

In 1812, a new war broke out between the United States and Great Britain. The conflict was a disaster in almost every respect for the ill-prepared Americans. But it ended on a high note, thanks to Jackson. Sporting the nickname "Old Hickory" (hickory being a notoriously hard wood) and commanding a hastily assembled army at New

Orleans, Jackson won a terrific victory over a British invasion force in 1815. That victory made Jackson the most celebrated man in America.

By 1824, Jackson was ready for a run at the presidency. His two most serious opponents were the Speaker of the House, Henry Clay, and the secretary of state, John Quincy Adams.

Jackson won the popular vote but did not secure a majority in the Electoral College, which, according to the Constitution, threw the election into the House of Representatives. There, Clay's sudden endorsement of Adams swung the chamber and the presidency to Adams.

An infuriated Jackson, convinced that Adams and Clay had colluded against him in a "corrupt bargain," declared his intention to run again in 1828. This time he beat Adams in a landslide.

As president, he applied his characteristic ruthlessness to the federal budget, slashing infrastructure projects he did not believe were the province of the national government. When the national bank came up for recharter in 1832, he vetoed it.

Jackson, who harbored a lifelong distrust of bankers, insisted that the nation's assets should be distributed to financial institutions throughout the United States rather than concentrated in one location. Was he right? No. This decision led to the financial depression of 1837. But Jackson never doubted himself. That was Jackson.

Old Hickory's most controversial decision came in 1830. The issue was tariffs. South Carolina, represented by Jackson's own vice president John Calhoun, insisted that tariffs be lowered because they favored manufacturing and commercial interests at the expense of Southern plantations. Calhoun assumed Jackson, a Southern planter himself, would agree. Otherwise, Calhoun warned, South Carolina would assert its state sovereignty and nullify the collection of federal tariffs within its boundaries.

But Jackson regarded South Carolina's nullification threat as an attack on the Constitution—and on his authority as president. The states had voted themselves into a federal union in 1788, Jackson insisted, and no single state or group of states could defy it.

Back down or face the wrath of the United States military, Jackson told South Carolina. He even threatened to "hang the first man of them I can get my hands on to the first tree I can find!"

South Carolina backed down.

Significant as Jackson's triumph was at the time, it was even more so thirty years later. It bolstered President Lincoln's argument that the Southern states had no constitutional right to secede from the Union.

If Jackson believed there could only be one national authority within America's borders, where did that leave the Indian tribes and their separate nations? No place good. In 1830, Jackson relentlessly pushed an Indian removal bill through Congress, requiring the Cherokee and other tribes in Georgia, Alabama, and Florida "to emigrate beyond the Mississippi."

The Cherokee appealed to the United States Supreme Court and won, but Jackson waved away the court's authority, and forced the tribes westward in a dreary exodus that became known as the Trail of Tears. That was Jackson.

Judge Jackson favorably or harshly (Jackson, by the way, wouldn't care).

But no one can deny the outsize role he plays in American history.

Allen Guelzo is a bestselling author, distinguished American historian, and commentator on public issues. He is a professor of humanities at the University of Florida. Before that, he was the Thomas W. Smith Distinguished Research Scholar and director of the James Madison Program Initiative on Politics and Statesmanship at Princeton University.

He is the first two-time winner of the coveted Lincoln Prize for his books *Abraham Lincoln: Redeemer President* and *Lincoln's Emancipation Proclamation*. His other books include *Robert E. Lee: A Life*, *Gettysburg: The Last Invasion*, and his newest book, *The Golden Thread: A History of the Western Tradition*. He has written for the *New York Times*, the *Washington Post*, the *Los Angeles Times*, the *Wall Street Journal*, the *Christian Science Monitor*, *U.S. News & World Report*, and *National Review*, and has been featured on NPR's *Weekend Edition Sunday*, *Meet the Press*, and Brian Lamb's *Booknotes*.

He holds an M.A. and Ph.D. in history from the University of Pennsylvania.

CHAPTER 9

MARTIN VAN BUREN

Political Magician

By Wilfred McClay

Think for a moment about the word "politician." What does it mean to you? Is it a term of praise?

That seems unlikely.

Instead, words like "partisan" or "corrupt" probably spring to mind.

Many of America's Founding Fathers felt the same way. They hoped the nation could be governed without political parties, by citizen-statesmen who transcended their differences for the sake of the public good.

But that ideal proved hard to establish, and even harder to maintain.

As the country grew, the economic and political interests of different groups diverged, and disagreements over various issues—taxes, westward expansion, slavery—widened so much that they couldn't be smoothed over by simple appeals to patriotism.

The first American leader to embrace this reality was Martin Van Buren, the eighth president of the United States—the first president who deserves to be called a professional politician.

Van Buren recognized that political conflict was unavoidable. The trick, he realized, was to make sure you had an organization to protect your interests. Thus, the significance of his crowning achievement—the forging of the Democratic Party. This was his vehicle for promoting the political ideals of the Founding Father he most admired, Thomas Jefferson, and those of the charismatic general with whom he became so closely associated, Andrew Jackson.

Their ideals—the preeminence of state and local concerns, the suspicion of a national bank that catered to Eastern elites, and the wisdom of limiting the power of the federal government—were the heart of his political convictions.

Yes, as odd as it sounds now, the Democratic Party, in Van Buren's day, was the party of small government.

Martin Van Buren was born on December 5, 1782, in the upstate New York town of Kinderhook, where his father ran a popular inn and tavern located on the road between New York City and Albany. Tavern life offered the young man an advanced course in political science. Current events were, so to speak, on the menu every day. His tavern experience also helped him understand what made people tick and how to deal with them.

In 1796, at age thirteen, he apprenticed to a local attorney and learned the basic rudiments of the legal profession. The practice of law became his ladder of upward mobility, and his entrée into the political world.

He also learned how to dress properly. More than that, he became renowned for his sartorial splendor, sometimes combining colors—yellow, orange, green, and brown—and fabrics—silk, velvet, and Moroccan leather—in a single ensemble.

But if his clothes were elite, his political leanings were not.

As he said in his memoirs, he had "faith in the capacity . . . of the People of our Country to govern themselves. . . ."

Van Buren's first political victory came in 1812 when he was elected to the New York State Senate. What he found there was—in a word—chaos: men with strong opinions, but unable to marshal them into effective political action.

Over the next decade, he went to work, melding his like-minded colleagues into a cohesive unit. To achieve his goals, he used the power of patronage (to offer jobs to supporters), the power of the press (to influence public opinion), and the power of the purse (to direct money to favored projects). Most importantly, he imposed discipline. If you were a party member, you supported the party. And if you didn't, the party wouldn't support you.

The political machine he created—the first in American history—was called the Albany Regency. With it, Van Buren dominated New York state politics for twenty years and earned the sobriquet "The Little Magician." He took his magic show national when he was elected to the US Senate in 1821.

But Van Buren's career really took off when he formed an alliance with military hero Andrew Jackson.

The combination of Jackson's popular appeal and Van Buren's organizational genius made them a formidable duo. With Van Buren as a top advisor, Jackson decisively won the 1828 and 1832 presidential elections. Van Buren became Jackson's most trusted lieutenant. He served as Jackson's secretary of state, minister to the United Kingdom, and, in Jackson's second term, as vice president and designated heir.

In 1836, on the strength of Jackson's endorsement, Van Buren won the presidency for himself.

Ironically, Van Buren the professional politician turned out not to be very successful as president. The growing division of opinion over slavery and westward expansion made it difficult for Van Buren to work his usual magic and build consensus. But in the end, it was his inability to prevent the great banking Panic of 1837 and its resulting economic depression that cost him reelection in 1840.

So we are left with this paradox. Van Buren was America's first politician president but was far better at political organizing than he was at presidential leadership. Still, he left an important legacy that often goes unrecognized: the power that can be wielded by a well-organized and disciplined political party.

Wilfred McClay holds the Victor Davis Hanson Chair in Classical History and Western Civilization at Hillsdale College. Before coming to Hillsdale in the fall of 2021, he was the G. T. and Libby Blankenship Chair in the History of Liberty at the University of Oklahoma, and the director of the Center for the History of Liberty.

His book *The Masterless* received the 1995 Merle Curti Award of the Organization of American Historians. Among his other books are *The Student's Guide to U.S. History*, *Religion Returns to the Public Square*, and *Land of Hope*.

He served for eleven years on the National Council on the Humanities, the advisory board for the National Endowment for the Humanities, and is currently a member of the US Commission on the Semiquincentennial.

He is a graduate of St. John's College and received his Ph.D. in history from Johns Hopkins University.

CHAPTER 10

WILLIAM HENRY HARRISON

President for Thirty-One Days

By Richard Lim

The 1840 presidential election featured one of the most famous political slogans in American history. You may have heard of it: "Tippecanoe and Tyler, too!"

The "Tyler" of the slogan was John Tyler, the vice presidential candidate.

But who was Tippecanoe?

It wasn't a person. It was the site of a famous battle. The general who won that battle was William Henry Harrison, the man who became the ninth president of the United States.

Born into a leading Virginia family on February 9, 1773, his father, Benjamin Harrison V, was one of the fifty-six men who signed the Declaration of Independence.

William, the youngest of seven children, grew up on the family's large estate. But when his father died suddenly, the cushy life of his youth quickly became a memory. Like most Virginia planters, the estate was more debt than profit. And at eighteen, William was on his own.

He joined the army and was posted to the Northwest Territory—an area that includes what is now Ohio, Indiana, Illinois, Michigan, Wisconsin, and Minnesota.

Harrison quickly established himself as a brave soldier and competent administrator. In 1801, when Harrison was just twenty-seven, President John Adams appointed him governor of the entire region—an office Harrison would hold for twelve years.

As governor, Harrison was a passionate promoter of westward expansion. He negotiated seven treaties with the tribes of the region, acquiring about 50 million acres of land for the United States in the process.

While many of the Indians adapted to changing circumstances and melded into the new settlements and towns, some refused to. These gathered under the banner of the Shawnee chief Tecumseh.

In November 1811, Tecumseh's warriors, led by his brother Tenskwatawa, launched a surprise attack on Harrison's forces near the Tippecanoe River in what is now Indiana. After taking initial losses, Harrison and his men turned the tide and emerged victorious. The Battle of Tippecanoe made Harrison a national hero.

But his greatest triumph was yet to come.

And Tecumseh was again his nemesis. During the War of 1812 the Indian chief aligned himself with the British. At the Thames River near modern Detroit, the two forces faced off. Harrison prevailed. Tecumseh died in the battle. The victory provided a major morale boost for the American people during a war in which victories were few and far between.

His hero status secured, Harrison settled in North Bend, Ohio. He capitalized on his military record to get himself elected to Congress in 1816 and then to the Senate in 1824.

By 1829, the American political landscape had dramatically changed. The founding generation was gone, and the era of modern political parties had begun. Politics was no longer a game for the elites. As the population of the country grew and voting rights expanded, the "common man" demanded to be heard.

The man who recognized this better than anyone was the new president, Andrew Jackson. The hero of the Battle of New Orleans wrote the political playbook of the nineteenth century: the rough man of humble beginnings rises against all odds to great heights.

Jackson's political opponents, the Whigs, fought him throughout his two presidential terms, and got nowhere. But when Jackson stepped down in 1837, and his vice president, Martin Van Buren, took the top spot, the Whigs saw their chance. It also helped that the country had fallen into a major financial crisis: the Panic of 1837.

Taking a page out of Jackson's playbook, the Whigs turned to Harrison, who, like Jackson, was a military hero.

But that wasn't quite enough. They had to rewrite Harrison's biography. No longer was he a Virginia patrician. Now he was a hard-drinking log cabin frontiersman.

The strategy worked. The sixty-eight-year-old Harrison easily defeated Van Buren in the 1840 election, becoming the first Whig president. He was also, at that time, the oldest man to reach the highest office.

Eager to prove that he was hardy enough to do the job, he insisted on delivering a two-hour-long inaugural address—to this day, the longest ever given—without a hat, coat, or gloves on a freezing March afternoon.

In that speech, he offered his vision of a more modest presidency, in sharp contrast to Jackson's "my way or the highway" approach. Harrison vowed not to lord the presidential veto over Congress as Jackson had done.

Harrison had the makings of a successful president. He put together an all-star cabinet, featuring the great statesman Daniel Webster as his secretary of state. He called Congress into special session to deal with the economic crisis. He was no pushover. When Henry Clay, the "big wig" of the Whig Party, challenged his leadership, Harrison responded, "You forget, Mr. Clay, that I am the President."

But he wasn't for long.

That record-breaking inauguration speech may have been his undoing. Within weeks, he developed pneumonia. His condition worsened, and he died on April 4, 1841—exactly one month after being sworn in.

He was the first president to die in office and remains the shortest-serving chief executive in American history.

Richard Lim is the cofounder and host of the *This American President* podcast. The success of his podcast landed him interviews with several prominent guests, including former CIA and NSA Director Michael Hayden, Apollo 13 astronaut Fred Haise, Secret Service Agent Clint Hill, and FOX News host Bret Baier.

Lim has previously served at the White House, the Association of the US Army, and George Washington's Mount Vernon estate. He regularly appears on the nationally syndicated radio show *Point of View's Millennial Round Table.*

Lim's opinion editorials have appeared in the Daily Signal, the *Washington Examiner,* RealClearHistory, and the History News Network. Lim obtained a master's degree in public administration from Syracuse University's Maxwell School and a bachelor's degree from the University of California, San Diego.

CHAPTER 11

JOHN TYLER

President Without a Party

By Jared Cohen

A loud, persistent rapping woke United States Vice President John Tyler out of a sound sleep.

Clad in his sleeping frock and a cloth hat, an irritated Tyler opened the door. Two young men stood before him.

One of them handed the vice president a document.

Tyler broke the seal and read.

"My God, the President is dead."

The president was William Henry Harrison. He had been in office for only thirty-one days.

In America's short history, this had never happened before. And no one, including the vice president, was quite sure what to do.

It was April 1841.

John Tyler, tall, thin, with an aquiline nose and regal bearing, was the quintessential Southern gentleman. A longtime fixture in Virginia politics, he had served both as governor and senator. When Harrison, who was looking for someone to shore up his Southern base, offered him the VP slot, Tyler felt duty bound to accept.

The two men rode to an easy victory on the catchy slogan—one of the most memorable in presidential politics—"Tippecanoe and Tyler, too." ("Tippecanoe" referred to Harrison's 1811 victory over hostile Indians at the Tippecanoe River in Indiana.)

On March 4, 1841, Harrison gave a rambling two-hour inauguration speech on a cold, rainy afternoon. Soon after, Tyler left town and returned to his plantation. He figured he could be vice president there just as well as he could in Washington, and a lot more comfortable.

It was at Tyler's plantation that the messengers had delivered their fateful news.

When Tyler arrived in the nation's capital, the only person who assumed that he was now president was Tyler.

Here's why:

Article II of the Constitution reads as follows: "In Case of the Removal of the President from Office, or of his Death, Resignation, or Inability to discharge the Powers and Duties of the said Office, the Same shall devolve on the Vice President."

What does that mean?

It could easily mean that the vice president was just a placeholder until a new president could be chosen by Congress or by a special election. That's what John Quincy Adams, the former president and now Massachusetts congressman, believed. And many agreed with him.

Tyler took a decidedly different view.

If possession is nine-tenths of the law. Tyler had possession. And he wasn't going to let go.

Thus, a historical precedent was forever established: in the event of the death of the president, the vice president serves out the remaining term. We take this smooth transition for granted now, but only because of what Tyler did.

His first crisis solved, he immediately stepped into another.

Tyler was a member of the Whig Party. The Whigs were formed to oppose the Democrats, which had been created and dominated by the seventh president of the United States, Andrew Jackson. The big issue for the Whigs was the establishment of a national bank, which they saw as a way to get cheap credit to farmers to finance westward expansion. The Democrats, taking their lead from Jackson, hated the idea of giving power to what they believed were corrupt New York money interests.

Tyler, even though he was a Whig, disliked the idea of a national bank as much as Jackson did. When Congress, then dominated by the Whigs, passed a national bank bill, Tyler vetoed it—twice. The Whigs were so incensed, they kicked Tyler out of the party.

By his second year in office, he was a president without a party.

One could fairly ask, why, if Tyler opposed a national bank, was he a Whig at all. The answer reveals both the strength and weakness of that party. The strength was that it was a catchall for anyone who didn't like the Democrats—this included, oddly enough, both Northern abolitionists and Southern slave owners like Tyler. Abraham Lincoln, it should be remembered, was elected to Congress as a Whig. The weakness of the party was that it had no unifying platform. No two members could agree on any one thing—except that they hated the Democrats, of course.

Tyler thought he could use this confusion to his advantage to win a second term. His plan depended on achieving one enormous goal, bringing the Lone Star Republic of Texas into the United States. Texas, Tyler believed, would unite Whigs who favored westward expansion and Southern Democrats who liked the idea of adding a new slave state.

Tyler came close to pulling it off, but was thwarted not by anything he did, but by a freak naval accident that killed his chief negotiator on the Texas issue.

After his Texas plans fell apart, Tyler withdrew from the 1844 race. James Polk, his successor, a Tennessee Democrat, got the Texas glory.

Tyler returned to Virginia. But he wasn't finished with politics or history.

He was a passionate "states' rights" man. He believed the Tenth Amendment to the Constitution prohibited the federal government from interfering with slave ownership. Ultimately, he supported secession. In 1861, he was elected to the Congress of the Confederate States.

He died a year later, a traitor to the Union—his legacy forever tarnished.

Jared Cohen is cohead of the Office of Applied Innovation and president of Global Affairs at Goldman Sachs. Prior to joining the firm, Cohen was chief executive officer of Jigsaw, which he founded at Alphabet Inc. in 2016. From 2006 to 2010, he served as a member of the secretary of state's Policy Planning Staff and as a close advisor to both Condoleezza Rice and Hillary Clinton.

Cohen is a *New York Times* bestselling author of six books, including *Accidental Presidents*, *One Hundred Days of Silence*; *The New Digital Age*, which he coauthored with Eric Schmidt; and *Life After Power*. His writing has appeared in the *New York Times*, the *Wall Street Journal*, *Foreign Affairs*, the *Los Angeles Times*, the *Washington Post*, *Time*, and *Foreign Policy*.

Cohen is an Adjunct Senior Fellow at the Council on Foreign Relations and the Center for a New American Security.

CHAPTER 12

JAMES K. POLK

Manifest Destiny

By Wilfred McClay

What does the name James K. Polk mean to you?

Probably not much, if anything at all.

That's a shame, especially considering all he accomplished in just four years, from 1845 to 1849.

As the eleventh president of the United States, he acquired the Oregon Territory from the British, carried out the annexation of Texas, and then waged a successful war with Mexico that ended with the US acquiring California and the Utah and New Mexico territories. In doing so, he increased the nation's size by a third—transforming America into a truly continental nation, from sea to shining sea. Just look at a map of the United States. We have Polk to thank for much of it.

You'd think he'd have his own monument in Washington, DC.

And that's not all he did as president. He reduced taxes, stimulated the economy, and reformed the government's banking practices. Plus the California Gold Rush of 1848 made his acquisition of the Golden State look like a stroke of genius.

Born on November 2, 1795, young James grew up marinating in the politics of his father, Samuel Polk, a Tennessee county judge and a devoted follower of Thomas Jefferson. Samuel saw the world as a struggle between the virtuous farmer and the crafty banker; the city versus the country; the common man versus the wealthy elite.

His son James never strayed far from this worldview.

After graduating with honors from the University of North Carolina in May 1818, Polk moved to Nashville. There he established a law practice and, like so many ambitious young men of his day, used his legal career as a springboard into politics. He was elected to the Tennessee state legislature in 1823.

There he came to the attention of General Andrew Jackson, the hero of the War of 1812. The two men formed a father-son bond that became so close that Polk earned the nickname "Young Hickory" to Jackson's "Old Hickory."

Polk got himself elected to the US Congress in 1825, shortly after Jackson had lost to John Quincy Adams in one of the most controversial presidential elections in American history. Polk proved his loyalty to the general by becoming a persistent thorn in Adams's side.

When Jackson came roaring back to win the presidency in 1828, Polk was right there with him, as an advisor and confidant. As a Jackson insider, Polk rose quickly, becoming the chairman of the influential Ways and Means Committee, then Speaker of the House, then governor of Tennessee. It seemed that every political door was opening to him.

Then, suddenly, it all went south.

Running for reelection as governor in 1841, Polk lost to an obscure, somewhat buffoonish Whig opponent, James "Lean Jimmy" Jones. Polk may have won on the issues, but his six-foot-two-inch 125-pound opponent won on crowd-pleasing humor. That was bad enough, but when Lean Jimmy beat Polk again in 1843, everyone assumed that Polk's once-promising political career was over.

Then, one year later, in 1844, everything changed again.

The reason was Texas.

The new Republic of Texas had achieved its independence from Mexico in 1836 and had been seeking to become part of the United States ever since.

Fearing a war with Mexico, Congress wavered on Texas annexation for almost a decade. By 1844, however, American public opinion, bursting with expansionist fever, had undergone a massive shift in favor of annexation.

Both Martin Van Buren, the likely Democratic nominee, and Henry Clay, the likely Whig nominee, misread the national mood. They publicly stated that they would oppose the annexation of Texas. They didn't realize it at the time, but this doomed their campaigns and cleared the way for a pro-annexation candidate. That candidate turned out to be

Polk, who beat Van Buren for the Democratic nomination and then Clay for the presidency.

At the age of forty-nine, Young Hickory became the youngest president the country had ever had. In the course of just a few months, he had gone from the humiliation of defeat to the shining prize of the White House.

His term of office will always be closely identified with the mid-nineteenth-century idea of "Manifest Destiny"—the belief that the American democracy should extend from coast to coast, enveloping the entire continent.

And that may be why today we don't always give him the credit he deserves. We tend to see Manifest Destiny in negative terms, as a form of American imperialism, pure and simple. But Polk never saw it that way.

Along with most Americans of his day, the very ones who swept him into office, he was confident that what he was doing was noble and good, bringing freedom and prosperity across the continent to ever more people.

Looking back almost two centuries, isn't that exactly what he did?

Wilfred McClay holds the Victor Davis Hanson Chair in Classical History and Western Civilization at Hillsdale College. Before coming to Hillsdale in the fall of 2021, he was the G. T. and Libby Blankenship Chair in the History of Liberty at the University of Oklahoma, and the director of the Center for the History of Liberty.

His book *The Masterless* received the 1995 Merle Curti Award of the Organization of American Historians. Among his other books are *The Student's Guide to U.S. History*, *Religion Returns to the Public Square*, and *Land of Hope*.

He served for eleven years on the National Council on the Humanities, the advisory board for the National Endowment for the Humanities, and is currently is a member of the US Commission on the Semiquincentennial.

He is a graduate of St. John's College and received his Ph.D. in history from Johns Hopkins University.

CHAPTER 13

ZACHARY TAYLOR

The Man Who Might Have Prevented the Civil War

By Joseph Fornieri

Zachary Taylor, the twelfth president of the United States, was so indifferent to politics that he never voted until his own election in 1848.

A career military man, "Old Rough and Ready," as he was affectionately known, was weathered, stocky, and bow-legged in appearance. He was obstinate, easily insulted, and quick-tempered in character. These are not traits that usually make for a successful politician. But then again, he never wanted to be a politician. Until he did.

The son of a Revolutionary War veteran, Zachary Taylor was born in Orange County, Virginia, on November 24, 1784. Inspired by his father's military exploits, Taylor joined the army in 1808. He spent the bulk of the next forty years protecting the frontier against hostile Indians. Steadily rising from the rank of lieutenant to brigadier general, he fought in the War of 1812, the Black Hawk War of 1832, and the Second Seminole War in 1837.

The Mexican-American War in 1846 was a turning point in Taylor's life. In a matter of months, he went from a respected but obscure soldier to a national hero.

Here's how it happened.

In January 1846, President James Polk sent Taylor into the disputed border territory of Texas and Mexico. The idea was that the presence of American troops would pressure the Mexican government into accepting Polk's offer to buy California. But Mexico wasn't interested.

So Polk was stuck.

Things became unstuck when Mexican forces fired on Taylor's men near the town of Palo Alto, killing eleven. That's all Polk needed to ask Congress to declare war, which it did on May 12.

At that moment, the war rested on Taylor's shoulders. Despite being vastly outnumbered, he won the battle of Palo Alto and went on to score impressive victories at Monterrey and Buena Vista. Ulysses S. Grant, a recent West Point graduate who took part in the campaign, said of Taylor: "No soldier could face either danger or responsibility more calmly than he. . . . He was known to every soldier in his army, and was respected by all."

The Mexican-American War ended in February 1848, with the US acquiring not only California but vast swaths of land in the American Southwest. Within weeks of the end of the war, the Whig Party, which had done so well with war hero William Henry Harrison, saw Taylor as their ticket back to the White House.

Taylor was intrigued, but he didn't see himself as a party man. "I am a Whig, but not an ultra Whig," he said. "If elected I would not be the mere President of a party—I would endeavor to act independent of party. . . ."

That was good enough for the Whigs. In short order, they nominated Taylor to be their standard-bearer. He went on to defeat Lewis Cass, a Democratic senator from Michigan, in the general election.

Being a war general was hard. But being president was harder.

For one thing, the Mexican-American War had reignited the slavery debate. How would all this new territory be integrated into the Union? What part would be slave, what part would be free?

The political balance stood precariously at fifteen free states and fifteen slave states. Any additional states would tip the scales one way or the other. How would this be resolved?

If anyone was in a position to resolve it, Taylor seemed to be that man. Like many in the South, he was a slave owner. He owned plantations in Louisiana, Mississippi, and Kentucky with over three hundred slaves. Like many in the North, he opposed the expansion of slavery into the new territories. Furthermore, he was strongly pro-Union. When aggrieved Southerners threatened secession, Taylor bluntly informed them that he would hang any traitors "with less reluctance than . . . the deserters and spies in Mexico."

So what did Taylor do? Not what most expected him to do—certainly not his supporters in the South. He endorsed immediate statehood for California and New Mexico, both of which were likely to become free states.

As serious talk of civil war arose in Congress and across the country, an aging Henry Clay struggled to engineer one last grand bargain. Here, in part, is what he proposed: California would be admitted as a free state; the territories of New Mexico and Utah would decide for themselves whether to be free or slave; and to appease the South, the Fugitive Slave Act—requiring runaway slaves to be returned to their owners—would be strengthened.

Taylor would have none of it. First of all, he disliked Henry Clay. He thought that Clay never gave him the respect he felt he deserved. If Clay was for it, Taylor was against it. But second, he adamantly opposed the Fugitive Slave Act. Because of Taylor's opposition, Clay's grand bargain got nowhere.

And that's where things stood when Taylor died suddenly in the summer of 1850.

Had he lived, could he have found a way to bridge the gap between North and South, free and slave? We'll never know.

Joseph Fornieri is professor of political science at the Rochester Institute of Technology and the director of the Center for Statecraft, Law, and Liberty. He was also a member of the Lincoln Bicentennial Commission and a Fulbright Lecturer at Charles University in Prague, Czech Republic.

He is the author of several books on the sixteenth president, including *Abraham Lincoln's Political Faith* and *Abraham Lincoln, Philosopher Statesman*. His recent books include *Free Speech: Core Court Cases*, *Abraham Lincoln: Core Documents*, and *American Statesmanship: Principles and Practices of Leadership* from University of Notre Dame Press.

A former high school teacher, Fornieri conducts outreach to secondary teachers and students throughout the country. He is now working on a book comparing and contrasting the political thought and leadership of Abraham Lincoln and Frederick Douglass.

CHAPTER 14

MILLARD FILLMORE

The Last Whig President

By Jared Cohen

No one was more surprised than Millard Fillmore when the Whig Party chose him to be Zachary Taylor's running mate in the 1848 election.

Working as the comptroller (essentially the treasurer) of New York State at the time, Fillmore was well known in Washington. He had been a New York congressman for a decade. But the VP slot? Fillmore didn't see it coming.

And he didn't hesitate to say yes when offered the job.

On the surface, Taylor and Fillmore seemed to be a good fit.

Taylor had never run for elective office. He was the great hero of the Mexican-American War. When he wasn't soldiering, he lived on a plantation in the Deep South.

Fillmore, a Northerner, spent his professional life in politics.

Both had grown up on the edge of the frontier. Both were entirely self-made.

It was a marriage made in machine-politics heaven.

And it worked.

Well, to be more accurate, it worked for Taylor.

It didn't work for Fillmore.

When they won the 1848 election, Fillmore figured that as vice president he could dispense lucrative federal jobs to his supporters, securing his future as a major force in New York and maybe even national politics.

He also figured that with his knowledge of Congress and his vast experience in the political arena, he would be a trusted Taylor advisor.

He figured wrong on both counts.

Taylor gave him no access to patronage. He wasn't interested in boosting Fillmore's career in New York or anywhere else.

And Taylor did not bring Fillmore into his inner circle. The two men didn't even meet until after the election. And when they did, they didn't much like each other. It seems that their many differences on political issues, though assets during the campaign, were detriments after it. For example, Taylor, the Southerner, accepted slavery (though, to his credit, he did oppose its spread to new states), while Fillmore, the Northerner, opposed slavery.

Fillmore made one more miscalculation.

He never thought Taylor would die in office.

After dedicating the base of the Washington Monument on a very hot, humid day, Taylor returned to the White House with heat exhaustion. Then the doctors got ahold of him. In the mid-nineteenth century, this was not necessarily a good thing. Over the next few days, Taylor's health got worse. He died on July 9, 1850. The doctors, trying all manner of nostrums, including bleeding him from the wrist, effectively cured him to death.

Fillmore—thanks to the precedent John Tyler established ten years before—suddenly found himself the thirteenth president of the United States.

It would have been a difficult job for anyone.

On the one hand, thanks to victory in the Mexican-American War, a new treaty with Spain, and the rise of the Mormon community in Utah, the United States had in just the previous year almost doubled in size. Texas, California, New Mexico, Arizona, Utah, and Colorado would all eventually become states.

On the other hand, there was a burning question: Which would be free states, and which would be slave states?

During a four-hour speech, the aging lion of the Senate, Whig leader Henry Clay, proposed an omnibus bill that would settle all the issues.

But the Senate was so divided that agreement on a single bill proved impossible. Feelings ran so hot that on more than one occasion actual fistfights broke out on the Senate floor.

Fillmore, with the help of Illinois Senator Stephen Douglas, a

Democrat, came up with a practical solution: break the big bill into five separate parts. Each part could then be debated on its own merits.

This was known as the Compromise of 1850.

Here's how each piece broke down:

One: California would be admitted as a free state.

Two: The boundaries of Texas, already a slave state, were fixed.

Three: The New Mexico and Utah territories would be allowed to determine for themselves whether they would be free or slave.

Four: The slave trade would be abolished in Washington, DC.

Five: The right of Southern slave owners to recover runaway slaves in the North was enhanced.

Fillmore hated this last bill, the Fugitive Slave Act, but signed it anyway. He feared, with good reason, that if he didn't, the Southern states would bolt and the Union would be shattered. In other words, he feared Civil War.

History has not been kind to the Compromise of 1850, but at the time, the nation breathed a huge sigh of relief. Civil war had been averted, or so they thought.

If Zachary Taylor hadn't died in office, he would have almost certainly vetoed all or part of the five bills. But thanks to the pragmatic Millard Fillmore, they all crossed the finish line.

To get it done, Fillmore had alienated his own Whig Party, killing any chance he had of winning their presidential nomination in 1852. As it turned out, he was the last of the Whig line.

The party would dissolve over the coming decade, torn apart by internal disagreements. It would be replaced by a new, antislavery party with a much clearer vision of the future. They would call themselves Republicans.

Jared Cohen is cohead of the Office of Applied Innovation and president of Global Affairs at Goldman Sachs. Prior to joining the firm, Cohen was chief executive officer of Jigsaw, which he founded at Alphabet Inc. in 2016. From 2006 to 2010, he served as a member of the secretary of state's Policy Planning Staff and as a close advisor to both Condoleezza Rice and Hillary Clinton.

Cohen is a *New York Times* bestselling author of six books, including *Accidental Presidents*, *One Hundred Days of Silence*; *The New Digital Age*, which he coauthored with Eric Schmidt; and *Life After Power*. His writing has appeared in the *New York Times*, the *Wall Street Journal*, *Foreign Affairs*, the *Los Angeles Times*, the *Washington Post*, *Time*, and *Foreign Policy*.

Cohen is an Adjunct Senior Fellow at the Council on Foreign Relations and the Center for a New American Security.

CHAPTER 15

FRANKLIN PIERCE

A President in a Torn Country

By Joseph Fornieri

By all accounts, Franklin Pierce, the fourteenth president of the United States, was a fine person: charming, caring, deeply empathetic. These are all characteristics you want in a friend—and Pierce had many—but they don't necessarily make for a strong leader. Unfortunately, Pierce's appointment with history came when such a leader was sorely needed. Try as he might to fill the role, Pierce couldn't do it.

Franklin Pierce was born November 23, 1804, in Hillsborough, New Hampshire. Raised in the shadow of his prominent father, Benjamin, a Revolutionary War hero, Franklin began his political career shortly after graduating from Bowdoin College in 1824.

He was a political natural. In addition to his good looks, he was an eloquent speaker. Gifted with a photographic memory, he almost always spoke without notes, connecting directly to his audience. He won his first election in 1829 to the New Hampshire State Legislature. In 1832, he was elected to Congress, and by 1837, he was a US senator, the youngest member at the time.

The overriding political issue of the day was slavery. To understand Pierce, we need to understand his position on this issue. While not a slave owner himself, Pierce believed that the Constitution committed the federal government to protecting slavery. Not surprisingly, Pierce's position endeared him to his Southern colleagues. This support was key to his political career.

By 1842, Pierce was ready to leave Washington. He needed to make more money and care for his chronically ill wife. He did both without ever truly leaving politics. In fact, he became more influential during this period by becoming the Democratic Party boss of his home state of New Hampshire. He might have happily stayed there were it not for the outbreak of the Mexican-American War in 1846.

The Americans won that war decisively, acquiring vast new territories in the West, including California. But the victory also had the unintended consequence of stirring up the slavery issue. What would happen to these new territories? Would they become slave or free?

After fierce debates, the Compromise of 1850 resolved the issue—or so it seemed. California would be admitted into the Union as a free state while the status of the new territories of New Mexico and Utah would be determined at a later, unspecified time. And that's where things stood when Franklin Pierce, through an improbable series of circumstances, became America's fourteenth president.

When the Democratic Convention opened in June 1852 in Baltimore, Pierce was not even a dark horse candidate; he wasn't a horse at all. But when the convention repeatedly deadlocked between Michigan Senator Lewis Cass; former Secretary of State James Buchanan; and Illinois Senator Stephen Douglas, the mastermind of the Compromise of 1850, Pierce saw his chance. On the convention's forty-ninth ballot, Pierce emerged as the compromise candidate everyone North and South could get behind. With the opposition party, the Whigs, hopelessly divided between their own Northern and Southern wings, Pierce easily took the White House.

Pierce's goal for his presidency was to do everything he could to keep the Democratic Party united and the country calm. As modest as this sounds, it proved very difficult to achieve.

To keep his party united, he appointed Northerners and Southerners to key government posts. Jefferson Davis of Mississippi, for example, was his secretary of war, and Caleb Cushing, a Massachusetts moderate, was his attorney general. To keep the country calm, Pierce strongly endorsed the Compromise of 1850.

And then one Sunday in January 1854, it all began to unravel.

Stephen Douglas showed up at the White House with a new idea he promised would resolve the slavery issue once and for all. It was deceptively simple: let new territories—future states—determine by popular vote—Douglas called this "Popular Sovereignty"—whether they would be slave or free. This principle became the core of the Kansas-Nebraska

Act, perhaps the most disastrous piece of legislation in American history. It repealed the Missouri Compromise of 1820 that banned slavery above latitude 36°30', thereby opening up the rest of the Louisiana Territory to slavery. And it shattered the tenuous peace achieved by the Compromise of 1850.

Almost immediately, anger, often violent, exploded across Kansas, across Congress, and across the nation, as both sides—free and slave—battled to control that state's destiny. From 1854 on, in a glimpse of the conflagration to come, "Bleeding Kansas" was a virtual war zone.

Why did Pierce agree to Douglas's plan and help him push it through Congress? One answer is that Douglas was the stronger personality. Pierce simply lacked the fortitude to say no. But there's a second possible answer: Pierce sincerely believed that the Kansas-Nebraska Act would work and reunite the country. It did just the opposite, of course, and it cost him a second term. He couldn't even win his party's nomination in 1856.

Four years and one more failed president later, the country would be engulfed in a catastrophic war. It would take an entirely different kind of leader to save the nation.

Joseph Fornieri is professor of political science at the Rochester Institute of Technology and the director of the Center for Statecraft, Law, and Liberty. He was also a member of the Lincoln Bicentennial Commission and a Fulbright Lecturer at Charles University in Prague, the Czech Republic.

He is the author of several books on the sixteenth president, including *Abraham Lincoln's Political Faith* and *Abraham Lincoln, Philosopher Statesman*. His recent books include: *Free Speech: Core Court Cases*, *Abraham Lincoln: Core Documents*, and *American Statesmanship: Principles and Practices of Leadership* from University of Notre Dame Press.

A former high school teacher, Fornieri conducts outreach to secondary teachers and students throughout the country. He is now working on a book comparing and contrasting the political thought and leadership of Abraham Lincoln and Frederick Douglass.

CHAPTER 16

JAMES BUCHANAN

A Legacy of Failure

By Joseph Fornieri

James Buchanan should have been prepared to be president. He had served as a congressman, a senator, a cabinet member, and an ambassador. He certainly wanted the job. He sought the office four times.

But when he finally achieved his ambition in 1856 and became the fifteenth president of the United States, his impressive résumé did him little good. When he left office in 1861, the country was on the brink of civil war.

James Buchanan was born in a log cabin on April 23, 1791, in Cove Gap, Pennsylvania. His Irish-born father, James Sr., lived the classic early-nineteenth-century immigrant story: he worked hard, lived frugally, and prospered. He and his American-born wife, Elizabeth, had great ambitions for their son, James Jr., and with the exception of a few stumbles—like getting kicked out of college for drunkenness—he didn't disappoint them.

Pursuing a legal career, young James moved to Lancaster, Pennsylvania, where he took a strong interest in local affairs. Elected to Congress in 1820 as a Federalist, he switched his allegiance to the newly formed Democratic Party in 1824, becoming a devoted follower of Andrew Jackson.

He supported states' rights and a strict reading of the Constitution, and was sympathetic to Southern interests, including, of course, slavery. Northerners with such inclinations were known by their political opponents as "doughfaces," men who were overly deferential to Southern grievances. Buchanan was more than happy to return the insult. He despised Northern abolitionists who, he believed, threatened the stability of the Union with their "extremist" views.

In 1844, he took his first run at the Democratic presidential nomination. He lost to former Tennessee Governor James Polk. In 1848, he lost to Michigan Senator Lewis Cass. In 1852, he lost yet again, this time to New Hampshire's Franklin Pierce. In 1856, the stars finally aligned. Buchanan won the Democratic nomination and then the presidency by defeating legendary explorer and abolitionist John Frémont of the newly formed, antislavery Republican Party.

If Buchanan is known for anything, it's that he was the only bachelor to become president. All the rumors you might have heard about his sexual orientation were common fodder even in his day. But there is no convincing evidence that the rumors were true.

When Buchanan took office, the country was a tinderbox, ready to explode over the issue of slavery.

Kansas, for example, had become a battleground between pro- and antislavery forces. The two sides were literally fighting and dying over control of the state's government.

Buchanan thought he had a way to extinguish the fire. His hopes rested on the outcome of a highly anticipated Supreme Court case, *Dred Scott v. Sandford.*

The dispute came down to this question: Did a former slave have standing to sue in federal court?

Buchanan actually knew the answer the court would give before the decision was publicly announced. Indeed, he had secretly pressured the court to rule in the way he wanted: slaves had no standing to sue in federal court.

That would've been bad enough, but Chief Justice Roger B. Taney, who wrote the majority opinion, went much further. He denied that blacks—even those already free—could ever be citizens of the United States. But it didn't stop there: Taney also ruled that the federal government had no right to restrict the spread of slavery. To Abraham Lincoln and others, this meant that slavery would no longer be confined to a particular region of the country but would become a national institution.

Buchanan assumed, now that the court had made its decision, the matter was closed.

But this was wishful thinking, in the extreme.

Instead of resolving the slavery issue, *Dred Scott* only inflamed it.

Then, in 1859, the match was lit. Radical abolitionist John Brown led an unsuccessful slave revolt in Harpers Ferry, Virginia. While many in the North hailed Brown as a hero and a martyr, the South regarded him as a dangerous terrorist. Southerners were now convinced that Northerners were plotting their destruction.

Meanwhile, Buchanan was caught in no-man's-land. Both sides of his own Democratic Party—the pro-unionist and pro-secessionist—saw him as weak and ineffectual. He did nothing to disprove that view. Although he declared secession unconstitutional, he likewise believed he had no authority to force the states to remain in the Union.

Exhausted, he had no trouble keeping his promise not to run for a second term.

Even so, the worst of his sins was yet to come.

Buchanan did almost nothing between November 1860 and March 1861, five impossibly long months before the newly elected Republican president, Abraham Lincoln, took office. The Southern states left the Union one by one, seizing federal property as they went—forts, customhouses, post offices, and armories.

In short, Buchanan allowed the South to arm itself for war.

That war would come soon enough.

Joseph Fornieri is professor of political science at the Rochester Institute of Technology and the director of the Center for Statecraft, Law, and Liberty. He was also a member of the Lincoln Bicentennial Commission and a Fulbright Lecturer at Charles University in Prague, the Czech Republic.

He is the author of several books on the sixteenth president, including *Abraham Lincoln's Political Faith* and *Abraham Lincoln, Philosopher Statesman*. His recent books include: *Free Speech: Core Court Cases*, *Abraham Lincoln: Core Documents,* and *American Statesmanship: Principles and Practices of Leadership* from University of Notre Dame Press.

A former high school teacher, Fornieri conducts outreach to secondary teachers and students throughout the country. He is now working on a book comparing and contrasting the political thought and leadership of Abraham Lincoln and Frederick Douglass.

CHAPTER 17

YOUNG ABE

From Log Cabin to White House

By Allen Guelzo

If the best of America could be embodied in one man, that man would be Abraham Lincoln, the sixteenth president of the United States.

Born on February 12, 1809, Lincoln lived his early years in a log cabin with a dirt floor. He described his childhood and adolescence in Kentucky and later Indiana in bleak terms, as "the backside of this world."

His father, Thomas Lincoln, didn't see much practical value in formal education, and his son received almost none.

But young Lincoln's instincts pointed in an entirely different direction. He devoured every book he could get his hands on. And aided by a near-photographic memory, he retained everything he read. His goal was always (what he called) "improvement."

At age nineteen, now six feet four inches tall, he worked on flatboats carrying cargo down the Mississippi River, finally settling as a store clerk in New Salem, Illinois. There, Lincoln quickly established a reputation for good humor, scrupulous honesty, and a fierce determination "to make the most of himself."

In 1832, following a stint in the state militia, he decided to pursue a legal career.

Like many lawyers, he was drawn to politics. In 1834, he won election to the state legislature.

Lincoln endorsed the tenets of the Whig Party, which had been organized by Senator Henry Clay as a breakaway from the dominant Democratic Party. Clay and the Whigs supported policies that would build national commercial infrastructure, like roads and canals; create a national bank to stimulate investment and expansion into the West; and build tariffs around struggling American industries to protect them from foreign competition.

For many Northern Whigs like Lincoln, slavery was also an issue; and in 1837, Lincoln made his first public statement against slavery, condemning it as "founded on injustice and bad policy."

In 1846, Lincoln was elected to Congress to represent the newly created Seventh District in central Illinois. What he hoped would be the start of a career in national politics quickly fizzled. Lincoln criticized President James Polk, a Democrat, for goading Mexico into war. It was a principled but unpopular stance and cost him reelection.

He returned to Illinois in 1849 at the end of his solitary term to devote himself to his law practice. He quickly established himself as one of the top attorneys in the state. His ability to master the facts of a case no matter how complex and then weave those facts into a coherent narrative—always leavened by his inexhaustible supply of funny stories—made him irresistible to juries.

But in 1854, he was pulled back into politics. The passage of the Kansas-Nebraska Act, which would open the door to the expansion of slavery into the new territories west of the Mississippi River, "aroused him," he said, "as he had never been before."

In 1856, Lincoln found a new political home with a new antislavery party, the Republicans. Running as a Republican for the first time, he contested the US Senate seat held by Illinois's favorite Democratic son, Stephen Douglas, who had authored the Kansas-Nebraska Act.

What was supposed to be an easy win for Douglas turned into a hard-fought campaign. In seven open-air debates across the state—sometimes before as many as fifteen thousand people—the two men hammered each other over the slavery issue. Lincoln narrowly lost the election but won wide recognition as a rising star.

His star burned even brighter after he gave a speech at Cooper Union in New York City. There, he articulated how the original intent of the Founders had been for the steady elimination of slavery.

The time had now come to act on that intent.

When the Republican National Convention met in Chicago in May 1860, it was assumed that William Seward, a prominent senator from New York, would be the party nominee. But Lincoln, to the delight of the "hometown" Illinois crowd, slipped past him on the third ballot.

The Democrats, in contrast, could not unite behind one candidate. They splintered into two factions, a moderate one led by Lincoln's old nemesis, Stephen Douglas, and a radical proslavery one led by John Breckenridge of Kentucky. Lincoln's victory was thus assured. On Election Day, November 6, 1860, Lincoln received only 39 percent of the popular vote, but 59 percent of the Electoral College.

The Southern states, however, refused to accept this outcome.

The civil war the country had avoided for six decades—through one compromise after another—could be avoided no longer.

The heavy burden of leading the nation through that war would fall on the broad shoulders of a man about whom few knew anything, but many would soon come to revere.

Allen Guelzo is a bestselling author, distinguished American historian, and commentator on public issues. He is a professor of humanities at the University of Florida. Before that, he was the Thomas W. Smith Distinguished Research Scholar and director of the James Madison Program Initiative on Politics and Statesmanship at Princeton University.

He is the first two-time winner of the coveted Lincoln Prize for his books *Abraham Lincoln: Redeemer President* and *Lincoln's Emancipation Proclamation*. His other books include *Robert E. Lee: A Life*, *Gettysburg: The Last Invasion*, and his newest book, *The Golden Thread: A History of the Western Tradition*. He has written for the *New York Times*, the *Washington Post*, the *Los Angeles Times*, the *Wall Street Journal*, the *Christian Science Monitor*, *U.S. News & World Report*, and *National Review*, and has been featured on NPR's *Weekend Edition Sunday*, *Meet the Press*, and Brian Lamb's *Booknotes*.

He holds an M.A. and Ph.D. in history from the University of Pennsylvania.

CHAPTER 18

ABRAHAM LINCOLN

The President We Needed

By Allen Guelzo

When Abraham Lincoln came to Washington in March 1861 following his election as the sixteenth president of the United States, he had no thought that the country would soon be embroiled in a costly and bloody civil war.

The slave states of the South had threatened secession in the past and always pulled back. This time, Lincoln believed, would be no different.

He was open to accommodation if it would avoid armed conflict.

But he was unshakable on one point.

Lincoln insisted that secession was a constitutional impossibility and that he was obligated by his presidential oath to defend the integrity of the United States.

So, when the Confederates launched their attack on Fort Sumter in Charleston, South Carolina, on April 12, 1861, Lincoln called up federal troops and declared a naval blockade of the southern coast.

The war was on.

And Lincoln was completely unprepared for it.

Everything went badly at first. A hastily assembled federal army met with a humiliating defeat at the first major battle of the war at Bull Run in Virginia.

More defeats followed.

But Lincoln stood firm. New armies were recruited; fresh funds were raised through taxes and bond sales; and the naval blockade was strengthened.

Gradually, the military tide turned. In the East, Union forces foiled an attempted invasion of Maryland and Pennsylvania at the bitter Battle of Antietam in September 1862, and a second Confederate invasion the following summer was smashed at the Battle of Gettysburg.

In the West, a federal naval flotilla seized the major Confederate port of New Orleans. This was followed by Union General Ulysses Grant's capture of the Confederate citadel on the Mississippi River at Vicksburg.

Lincoln saw in Grant a man who had the qualities to bring the war to a finish. In March 1864, he brought Grant to Washington to plan a major new offensive. Their plan was blunt, bloody, and effective: overwhelm the Confederacy with superior Union firepower. Grant pursued it relentlessly, aided by his equally relentless subordinate, William Tecumseh Sherman.

Lincoln rode the wave of Union victories to reelection in November 1864.

On April 9, 1865, the war finally came to a close with Lee surrendering to Grant at Appomattox Courthouse near Richmond, Virginia.

Lincoln rightfully deserves credit for his successful prosecution of the Civil War. What is less well known but nearly as significant are the major policy changes he introduced even while the war was being waged.

For six decades, the federal government had been dominated by the Democratic Party, and by its suspicion of commerce and manufacturing. Lincoln, however, had come to political maturity in the Whig Party, which favored the funding of transportation infrastructure to promote commerce, a national banking network to create a stable monetary system, and tariffs to protect American industries from foreign competition.

As president, Lincoln signed legislation that implemented all three of these new directions. This, along with his plan to create a transcontinental railroad, set the stage for the great industrial expansion of the United States during the last three decades of the nineteenth century.

And on January 1, 1863, he issued his Emancipation Proclamation that declared free all the slaves of the rebel Confederacy. This was the precursor to the Thirteenth Amendment to the Constitution in early 1865, forever outlawing slavery in the United States.

In all of these labors, Lincoln displayed astonishing resilience and humility in the face of both loss and victory. "I shall do nothing in malice," he wrote in 1862. He was true to his word.

By the start of his second term—the first of any president since Andrew Jackson—Lincoln had mastered every aspect of his office.

"The old man sits here," his personal secretary John Hay marveled, "and wields like a backwoods Jupiter the bolts of war and the machinery of government with a hand equally steady & equally firm."

His public addresses—especially his dedication remarks at the Soldiers' National Cemetery at Gettysburg in November 1863, and his second inaugural address, rose to levels of eloquence that no other president has matched.

Sadly, Lincoln had little time to savor his triumphs. On April 14, 1865—only five days after Lee's surrender—a fanatical Southern partisan, John Wilkes Booth, shot Lincoln from behind while the president was watching a play at Ford's Theatre in Washington.

Lincoln died the next morning without regaining consciousness.

All the world mourned.

Allen Guelzo is a bestselling author, distinguished American historian, and commentator on public issues. He is a professor of humanities at the University of Florida. Before that, he was the Thomas W. Smith Distinguished Research Scholar and director of the James Madison Program Initiative on Politics and Statesmanship at Princeton University.

He is the first two-time winner of the coveted Lincoln Prize for his books *Abraham Lincoln: Redeemer President* and *Lincoln's Emancipation Proclamation*. His other books include *Robert E. Lee: A Life*, *Gettysburg: The Last Invasion*, and his newest book, *The Golden Thread: A History of the Western Tradition*. He has written for the *New York Times*, the *Washington Post*, the *Los Angeles Times*, the *Wall Street Journal*, the *Christian Science Monitor*, *U.S. News & World Report*, and *National Review*, and has been featured on NPR's *Weekend Edition Sunday*, *Meet the Press*, and Brian Lamb's *Booknotes*.

He holds an M.A. and Ph.D. in history from the University of Pennsylvania.

CHAPTER 19

ANDREW JOHNSON

The President Who Wasn't Lincoln

By Allen Guelzo

It was April 1865. The Civil War was finally over. An exhausted, bloodied nation breathed a deep sigh of relief. . . .

Then, suddenly, shockingly, President Abraham Lincoln was dead, felled by an assassin's bullet while watching a play.

To take the reins of power at this tumultuous moment required a great man, a man of compassion, discernment, and discipline. Andrew Johnson, Lincoln's vice president, was not that man.

This is not to say he didn't have virtues. He did. He just didn't have the stuff it took to meet the moment.

Born into abject poverty on December 29, 1808, Johnson was apprenticed—"sold" would be more accurate—to a tailor at the age of ten. Legally bound to serve until he was twenty-one, he ran away after five years. He eventually settled in Greeneville, Tennessee, where he set up his own tailor's shop and prospered.

In 1834, he was elected mayor of Greeneville. From there, he climbed steadily up the political ladder: the state legislature in 1835, the US Congress in 1843, governor in 1853, and the Senate in 1857. He was still serving as US senator for Tennessee in 1861 when the Civil War broke out.

Although Johnson was a Democrat and a slave owner himself, when Tennessee left the Union to join the breakaway Confederacy and defend legalized slavery, Johnson denounced his state's secession on the floor of the Senate.

"I will not give up this Government," he thundered in December 1860. "No; I intend to stand by it, and I entreat every man throughout the nation who is a patriot . . . to come forward, that the Constitution shall be saved, and the Union preserved."

After Union military forces occupied large parts of Tennessee in

1862, Lincoln tagged Johnson as the state's provisional military governor. It was a shrewd move on the president's part: it demonstrated to Southerners and Democrats that they were welcomed as full partners with Lincoln's Republican Party in restoring the Union.

Johnson himself joined hands with Lincoln's policies by freeing his own slaves in 1863.

A Southern Democrat who could embrace the ending of slavery was exactly what Republicans hoped would draw Democratic voters to support Lincoln's reelection bid in 1864. The Republican nominating convention duly replaced Lincoln's original vice president, Hannibal Hamlin of Maine, with Johnson as Lincoln's running mate.

Johnson's career as vice president did not get off to a good start, to put it mildly. He showed up drunk at his—and Lincoln's—inauguration on March 4, 1865. Johnson had an excuse. He was seriously ill with what was probably typhoid fever. Unfortunately, he chose to medicate himself with whiskey.

No one dreamed that only six weeks later, the Confederacy would collapse, Lincoln would be dead from an assassin's bullet, and Johnson would become the seventeenth president.

At first, Johnson delighted the most radical members of Congress with promises that "treason must be made odious," and when Johnson's attorney general moved to indict several dozen of the high Confederate leadership for treason, it appeared as though Johnson would take a hard hand in reconstructing the Union.

It quickly became evident, though, that Johnson saw the South's plantation-owning and slave-owning elite as the sole cause of the Civil War; poor Southern whites were merely the victims of a "dangerous aristocracy" of plantation gentry, and he began handing out wholesale pardons to all but the most prominent Confederates.

His plan for Reconstruction required the Southern states to eliminate slavery, but Johnson saw no reason to extend voting rights, or many other rights, for that matter, to the freed slaves. When a baffled Congress tried to seize control by adopting civil rights and Reconstruction legislation of its own, Johnson vetoed their efforts.

Ultimately, the Republican majority overrode those vetoes and imposed a Reconstruction plan more favorable to the freed slaves. This only exacerbated the tension between Johnson and the legislative branch, and finally, in 1868, on the paper-thin pretext that he had illegally terminated one of his cabinet officers, Johnson was impeached by the House of Representatives; he missed conviction and removal by only one vote in the Senate.

By that point, however, his presidency was effectively finished. After the election of Ulysses Grant, Johnson returned to Tennessee, where he still enjoyed some popularity.

In January 1875, he staged a political comeback by winning election once more to the US Senate. But in July, he suffered a fatal stroke.

He was buried in Greeneville, wrapped (by his own request) in an American flag.

Allen Guelzo is a bestselling author, distinguished American historian, and commentator on public issues. He is a professor of humanities at the University of Florida. Before that, he was the Thomas W. Smith Distinguished Research Scholar and director of the James Madison Program Initiative on Politics and Statesmanship at Princeton University.

He is the first two-time winner of the coveted Lincoln Prize for his books *Abraham Lincoln: Redeemer President* and *Lincoln's Emancipation Proclamation*. His other books include *Robert E. Lee: A Life*, *Gettysburg: The Last Invasion*, and his newest book, *The Golden Thread: A History of the Western Tradition*. He has written for the *New York Times*, the *Washington Post*, the *Los Angeles Times*, the *Wall Street Journal*, the *Christian Science Monitor, U.S. News & World Report*, and *National Review*, and has been featured on NPR's *Weekend Edition Sunday*, *Meet the Press*, and Brian Lamb's *Booknotes*.

He holds an M.A. and Ph.D. in history from the University of Pennsylvania.

CHAPTER 20

ULYSSES S. GRANT

The General Who Saved the Union

By Garry Adelman

The year was 1862. America was in the depths of the Civil War.

Looking back, it's easy to believe that a Union victory was inevitable. The North had more money, more population, more industry.

But no one thought that at the time. In the first year of the war, it looked as if the South would win. A series of high-profile victories in the East convinced many that Confederates were better fighters, under better leaders.

Where would President Lincoln find a battlefield general who could do for the Union what Robert E. Lee was doing for the Confederacy—lead it to victory?

The man he found, the man who saved the Union, was Ulysses S. Grant. He wasn't Lincoln's first choice—or second, or third. In fact, when the war started in 1861, Lincoln had no idea who Ulysses S. Grant was. Hardly surprising, since at that time, Grant was selling hats to farmers' wives in a small town in Illinois.

His rise to glory is one of the most amazing stories in American history.

Born in Ohio on April 27, 1822, Grant had no ambition to be a soldier. His father pushed him into it, thinking he wasn't suited for much else. Grant's West Point career wasn't especially distinguished, either. But during the Mexican-American War (1846–1848), Grant proved himself to be an officer of unusual ability. He was cool under fire, daring, but rarely reckless. Even more important: the men under his command trusted him.

After that war, Grant returned to St. Louis to marry his fiancée, Julia Dent, the daughter of a slave-owning Missouri farmer. Grant was never happier than when he was with Julia. And he was never unhappier than when he was not. Unfortunately, in this period army life forced them to be separated, sometimes for many months.

To assuage his loneliness, Grant started to drink. While in a distant posting in Northern California a thousand miles from Julia, his drinking got the better of him. He resigned his army commission to avoid an embarrassing court-martial.

It was downhill from there, one business venture failing after another. By 1860, thoroughly humiliated with no money and no prospects, he was back working for his father in the small town of Galena, Illinois.

Then the Civil War happened.

The Union was in desperate need of experienced soldiers. Grant volunteered. His leadership skills were immediately obvious. He quickly advanced through the ranks.

In a little more than six months, he scored two major victories at Fort Henry and Fort Donelson, along the Tennessee and Cumberland Rivers. He followed these up with victory in the largest battle in American history up to that time—the Battle of Shiloh—making him a true Union hero in a cause that was starved for heroes.

There was nothing flashy about Grant's generalship. All he did was win.

Unlike the overly cautious generals that drove President Lincoln to distraction, Grant's battle plan was to always move forward, always put pressure on his foes. Any advantage the Union had in technology or manpower he employed to the fullest.

Like Napoleon, Grant was a superb reader of maps. He could identify the enemy's vulnerabilities and exploit them as he did in his brilliant 1863 Campaign for Vicksburg, a campaign that is still studied at war colleges.

In March 1864, Lincoln made Grant commander of all the Union armies. It took more than a year of the war's hardest fighting before Lee surrendered and the war finally came to an end.

By this point the president and his general had developed a close bond. Shortly after Grant returned to Washington, Lincoln invited the Grants to join him and Mary Lincoln at Ford's Theatre. Grant accepted. Julia, however, had developed an intense dislike for Mary Lincoln and insisted that her husband get out of the commitment. Embarrassed, Grant did.

That night in that theatre, Lincoln was assassinated.

As the commander of all Union armies, Grant was placed in a terrible bind, having to walk a tightrope between new president Andrew Johnson's pro-South agenda, which favored the old white aristocracy, and protecting, as Lincoln intended, the newly won rights of the freed slaves. He resolved his dilemma by deciding to run for president.

Grant had saved America once as a general. Could he save it again as a politician?

Running as the Republican candidate for president, Grant easily won the election in 1868, becoming the eighteenth president of the United States. He won again in 1872.

During his tenure, he fought to secure the passage of the Fifteenth Amendment, which guaranteed all American citizens the right to vote, regardless of "race, color, or previous condition of servitude."

He created the Department of Justice, broke up the Ku Klux Klan, and advocated for the rights of Indians.

He presided over the completion of the transcontinental railroad and a rapidly expanding industrial economy.

There was a dark side to his presidency, however. His administration was dogged by charges of financial impropriety, and he left office under a cloud. But Grant the man remained a popular figure.

Just days before his death on July 23, 1885, he completed his autobiography. It became one of the bestselling books of the nineteenth century.

Of Grant's amazing life, Frederick Douglass wrote a fitting epithet, "In him, the negro found a protector, the Indian a friend, a vanquished foe a brother, an imperiled nation a savior."

Garry Adelman is the vice president of the Center for Civil War Photography, director of History and Education for the Civil War Trust, and chief historian at the American Battlefield Trust.

Adelman is the award-winning author, coauthor, or editor of more than thirty books and articles on the Civil War. He authored *Gettysburg in 3-D*, *Antietam in 3-D*, *Manassas Battlefields Then & Now*, *The Civil War 150*, *Antietam: Then & Now*, and *The Myth of Little Round Top*. He has published articles in *Civil War*

Times, *Civil War Monitor*, *Gettysburg Magazine*, and *Hallowed Ground*. He has appeared as a speaker on the BBC, C-SPAN, and the History Channel, where he appeared on the Emmy Award–winning show *Gettysburg* and *Blood and Glory: The Civil War in Color*.

Adelman earned his B.A. in business from Michigan State University and his M.A. in history at Shippensburg University of Pennsylvania.

CHAPTER 21

RUTHERFORD B. HAYES

The Most Disputed President

By Jason R. Edwards

On election night 1876, Rutherford B. Hayes, the Republican candidate for president, went to bed firmly convinced he had lost.

Four months later, he walked into the White House as the nineteenth president of the United States. His ultimate victory remains the single most disputed presidential outcome in American history—more than *Bush vs. Gore* in 2000, more than *Trump vs. Biden* in 2020.

Hayes, the youngest of five children, was born on October 4, 1822, in a small town near Columbus, Ohio. His father had died two months earlier. His bachelor uncle, Sardis Birchard, a businessman and banker, became his guardian and surrogate father.

Like so many young Americans of his day, "Rud," as he was called, was imbued with a tireless work ethic. He was a conscientious student, graduating from Kenyon College in Ohio in 1842 at the top of his class. Thanks to his uncle's generosity, he graduated from Harvard Law School, where he also excelled.

By 1849, Hayes had started a successful law practice in the rapidly growing city of Cincinnati. Strongly opposed to slavery, he defended many runaway slaves in court.

When the Civil War broke out, Hayes was nearly forty, married, a father of three with a fourth on the way, and a leading figure in southern Ohio. He had everything to lose and nothing to gain by volunteering for the Union cause. But he did so anyway.

His leadership qualities were immediately recognized by his superiors and the soldiers under his command.

Hayes saw action at the Battles of Antietam, Winchester, and Cedar Creek, among others. Badly wounded in the first of those battles, he stayed on the field issuing orders. Had his men not carried him to safety, he would have died.

Entering the war without any military experience, he left it as a general. He also left it as a member of Congress, being elected by his fellow Ohioans in 1864.

In 1867, he resigned his congressional seat to run for governor of Ohio, his status as a war hero helping him carry the day.

After taking office in 1868, he pushed hard for black voting rights, first in his home state and then nationally by supporting the ratification of the Fifteenth Amendment. A popular governor, he was elected to two more terms.

With the 1876 election looming and the Grant administration mired in financial scandals, the party needed a candidate free of any taint of corruption—and Hayes fit the bill.

But the election was an uphill battle.

First, Hayes faced a formidable opponent, the Democratic governor of New York, Samuel Tilden.

Second, the Republican Party had been losing votes in the South because the Democrats were making it increasingly difficult for blacks to vote.

The election indeed turned out to be a photo finish. The *New York Times* reported that Tilden had won 184 electoral votes—just one vote short of victory—while Hayes captured 181. The wild cards were South Carolina, Louisiana, and . . . Florida.

Sound familiar?

A stalemate ensued, with each side bitterly accusing the other of cheating. Without any precedent or guidance from the Constitution, Congress set up a commission to settle the issue.

Finally, in February 1877, after some of the nastiest mudslinging in American history, the commission decided for Hayes. Congress ratified the decision on March 2. But many Democrats never accepted the result as legitimate and perpetually referred to Hayes as "Rutherfraud."

The big issue facing the new president was the status of the South.

The war had been over for twelve years. The Democrats desperately wanted federal troops to be recalled from the region. But those troops protected the rights of the freedmen.

Hayes had two choices: keep the troops in, or pull them out.

Hayes pulled them out, but only after securing assurances from the Southern governors that black voting and property rights would be protected. But perhaps he was naive. The governors largely failed to hold up their end of the bargain.

Should Hayes be blamed for the unsatisfactory results of Reconstruction and the subsequent rise of racist Jim Crow laws? He frequently is, but should he be? The country wanted to put the war behind it. There was little popular will for the occupation to continue, and it's doubtful that Congress would have consented to keeping federal troops in the South for much longer, no matter who was president.

It wasn't that Hayes was afraid to use force. He used it to put down a massive, nationwide rail strike in 1877, the first president to use the military in a labor dispute. But that was a specific, onetime action. Occupying a whole region of the country indefinitely was simply not sustainable.

Sectional issues were not Hayes's only concern. A committed advocate of civil service reform, he helped to restore honesty to government operations. And under his steady hand, the economy found its footing after suffering years of depression following the Panic of 1873.

In fact, Hayes seemed a shoo-in for reelection, except for one thing: he was committed to the idea that presidents should serve only one term. So despite any attempts to draft him, he adamantly refused. Afterward, he said, "Nobody ever left the Presidency with less regret [and] less disappointment[.]"

Jason Edwards is a professor of history at Grove City College and a Fellow for Popular Culture with the Institute for Faith & Freedom. He has published writings on history, culture, and education in a variety of newspapers and journals, including the *Washington Times*, the *University Bookman*, and *Touchstone*.

Edwards has served on the board of the Society for Classical Learning and was also instrumental in developing the classical studies minor offered at Grove City College.

A former Lehrman Scholar and Salvatori Fellow with the Intercollegiate Studies

Institute, Edwards's research interests center on agrarian philosophy and the history of learning in Western civilization. He coauthored the book *Ask the Professor: What Freshmen Need to Know.*

Edwards received his bachelor's degree from Asbury College and both his master's degree and doctorate from the University of Kentucky.

CHAPTER 22

JAMES GARFIELD

The Great President Who Never Was

By Louis Picone

In 1881, James Garfield became the second US president to be assassinated. But while Abraham Lincoln died a martyr sixteen years earlier for union and liberty, Garfield was killed for a less glorious cause: civil service reform.

While that doesn't seem like a big deal now, it was then. This was a time when most government positions were obtained through political connections.

This practice, known as "patronage" or the "spoils system," was the way both Republicans and Democrats held power. It created a lot of party loyalty—you owed your job to the party—but also led to a lot of incompetence and corruption.

Garfield was the first president to seriously challenge this system—he took on the party bosses who doled out jobs and instead appointed qualified civil servants on the basis of merit.

This courageous act cost America's twentieth president his life.

James Garfield was born on November 19, 1831, near Cleveland, Ohio.

His father died before James was two, leaving his strong-willed mother, Eliza, to raise him and his three siblings alone.

His mother and his older brother Thomas recognized that there was something special about James, and they made every possible sacrifice to get him an education.

James didn't disappoint them. He was an excellent student with an exceptional work ethic. It wasn't enough for him to merely master a subject. He had to be the best in his school. And invariably, he was.

He put himself through college by studying during the day and working as a janitor by night. The same year he graduated—1856—he joined the new antislavery Republican Party. A committed abolitionist, he got himself elected to the Ohio State Senate in 1859 at age twenty-eight.

When the Civil War began in 1861, Garfield abandoned politics to join the Union army.

As fate would have it, Garfield became one of the first major Union war heroes. He achieved that status by defeating Confederate forces at the Battle of Middle Creek in Kentucky in January 1862. Relative to future battles, it was a minor affair, but it was one of the first times that the Union could claim a victory, and it dispelled the notion that the South was invincible.

During the war, his fellow Ohioans elected him to the House of Representatives. Initially, Garfield felt uneasy about accepting the honor. He didn't want anybody to think he was running away from the battlefield. It took President Abraham Lincoln to convince him otherwise. Lincoln's argument was straightforward: he had enough generals; he needed more support in Congress.

It wasn't long before everyone recognized Garfield's manifold talents. He was a brilliant legislator, a master of details, and also known as the nicest person in Washington—too nice, many thought, to be considered presidential timber. Garfield had no ambitions to be president, so he didn't care. He was happy to rise to the chairmanship of the powerful Appropriations Committee and, eventually, House minority leader.

But his career path changed when the Republican Convention in 1880 deadlocked between former President Ulysses Grant and Maine Senator James G. Blaine.

Grant was backed by New York machine boss Senator Roscoe Conkling, a staunch defender of the spoils system.

Civil service reformers backed Blaine.

After thirty-three ballots, neither side could get the upper hand.

On the thirty-fourth ballot, almost out of nowhere, the Wisconsin delegation voted for Garfield. That was enough to get the ball rolling. Over the next two ballots, Garfield's delegate count skyrocketed to 399, enough to make him the party's nominee.

Nobody was more stunned than Garfield.

The general election was almost as dramatic. Garfield won by the slimmest of margins, defeating Democratic candidate Winfield Scott Hancock by a mere 8,000 votes out of 9 million cast. The electoral count, however, was decisive—214 to 155.

Boss Conkling assumed that Garfield, now in power, would just pay lip service to civil service reform.

He was wrong.

Garfield nominated pro-reform advocate William Robertson to run the New York Customs House—the motherlode of patronage, a position Conkling had long controlled.

Conkling was apoplectic. But his tantrum fell on deaf ears. It turned out that the boss's influence was less than he thought. The party backed the new president.

It was a major victory for Garfield and set up his first term for success. Not only did he establish presidential authority over party bosses and advance civil service reform—he could also advance civil rights for the former enslaved, something he desperately wanted to do.

And then there were issues about tariffs, the debt, and the currency for the president to deal with. Garfield was up for the task, but he never got the chance.

On July 2, 1881, a mentally unstable office seeker, Charles Guiteau, approached him and fired two shots.

The first grazed Garfield's arm. The second tore into his back.

Attempting to locate the bullet, doctors prodded their unwashed fingers and instruments into the president, infecting the area around the wound. Had they done nothing, he would have likely survived.

Two and a half months later, on September 19, Garfield died.

He had all the makings of a great president.

Would he have become one? We'll never know.

Louis Picone is the award-winning author of *Grant's Tomb: The Epic Death of Ulysses S. Grant and the Making of an American Pantheon*; *The President Is Dead! The Extraordinary Stories of the Presidential Deaths, Final Days, Burials, and Beyond*; and *Where the Presidents Were Born: The History & Preservation of the Presidential Birthplaces*.

Picone is a member of the Authors Guild, the American Historical Association, and the Ulysses S. Grant Monument Association, and is also a trustee on the board of the Grover Cleveland Birthplace Memorial Association. He holds a master's in history and teaches at William Paterson University.

Picone has spoken on the topic of presidential sites at the White House Historical Association Presidential Sites Summit, the James A. Garfield National Historic Site, and the Russian Academy of Sciences in Moscow. He has appeared on C-SPAN, the BBC, and NPR, and his writing has been published in *Time* and the *Washington Post.*

CHAPTER 23

CHESTER ALAN ARTHUR

The President Who Didn't Want to Be President

By Michael Knowles

When a *New York Times* reporter sought out Vice President Chester Alan Arthur to get a statement following the death of President James Garfield, Arthur's valet turned the reporter away. "He is sitting alone in his room," the valet explained, "sobbing like a child."

To be president of the United States was the last thing Arthur wanted. Vice president, a position with limitless privileges and almost no responsibilities, that was the job for him. And he was having a grand time of it until an assassin's bullet changed everything.

Garfield did not die immediately. There were days when it looked like he would recover, but then he would fade again. It didn't help that his doctors used their unwashed hands to try to recover bullet fragments.

When Garfield finally succumbed on September 19, 1881, Arthur had to face the music.

He was now the twenty-first president of the United States.

At least he looked the part. A fastidious dresser (he was known to try on twenty pairs of pants before choosing one), he cut an imposing figure. He was heavyset with a thick mustache and muttonchop sideburns.

Born in Fairfield, Vermont, on October 5, 1829, he was the fifth of nine children. His father was a preacher and committed abolitionist whose strong views on this subject forced him to move the family from town to town. Despite never being in one place for long, Arthur made friends easily. A conscientious student, he attended Union College, became president of the debate society, and pursued a law degree.

As a lawyer, Arthur took a lead role in major civil rights cases, including one that led to the desegregation of the New York City streetcar lines.

After the Civil War where he rose to the rank of brigadier general and distinguished himself as a quartermaster—the person responsible for getting supplies to the troops—he abandoned the law for politics. This pulled him into the orbit of notorious political boss New York Senator Roscoe Conkling. Arthur's loyalty to Conkling paid off when he was awarded the post of collector at the New York Customs House, a position that paid over $50,000 per year—more money than any federal officeholder, including the president.

Becoming vice president was, from a financial point of view, a step down. But it was a step up in prestige. He couldn't resist the temptation. Access to federal patronage—the chance to give cushy government jobs to his political friends—didn't hurt either.

But suddenly Arthur wasn't vice president anymore. He had the top job now.

And the job changed him.

In one of the least expected and most remarkable turnabouts in presidential history, the quintessential machine politician, a man who once bragged about vote buying, became the president who enacted the most sweeping civil service reform in fifty years. Much to the chagrin of his friends, most especially Conkling, he became an apostle of clean government and set the tone for future reforms that occurred after he left office.

The weight of the office had a deep effect on Arthur, but so did a remarkable correspondence he had with a young Manhattan invalid by the name of Julia Sand. For reasons that aren't entirely clear, she assiduously tracked Arthur's every move. Even more amazing, Arthur read her letters and took her advice to heart.

"Great emergencies awaken generous traits, which have lain dormant . . . ," she wrote him in one letter. "If there is a spark of true nobility in you, now is the occasion to let it shine. . . ."

And it did.

But civil service reform was only one of Arthur's achievements. Another was his passion to rebuild the American Navy, which had been woefully neglected since the Civil War. If the nation wanted to be a major player on the world stage, it needed a modern navy. Arthur asked for eleven new, state-of-the-art steel ships. Congress gave him four. It was a start.

Arthur also worked to protect the rights of Chinese immigrants. And true to his abolitionist upbringing, his policy toward blacks—he appointed a number of them to important government posts—was among the best of the post–Civil War presidents.

One aspect of Arthur's personality that did not change was his love of entertaining. The White House, which he insisted on redecorating (it was too drab), was party central. The menus were specially prepared by an imported French chef. Wine and spirits flowed freely. Nobody outdrank or outate the host.

Perhaps because of his lavish lifestyle, Arthur's health failed at the end of his term. In hindsight, it appears he suffered from Bright's, a terminal disease of the kidneys. Still, Arthur considered the idea of running for a second term. As a practical matter, his illness made this impossible. He would be a one-term president. He died two years after leaving office in November 1886, at age fifty-seven.

Arthur's contemporary, publisher Alexander McClure, summed up Arthur's tenure well. "No man ever entered the Presidency so profoundly and widely distrusted, and no one ever retired . . . more generally respected."

Michael Knowles is the host of *The Michael Knowles Show* at the *Daily Wire* and *The Book Club* at PragerU. He is also the bestselling author of *Reasons to Vote for Democrats*, which President Donald Trump hailed as "a great book for your reading enjoyment," and *Speechless: Controlling Words, Controlling Minds*.

In addition to podcast and radio, Knowles appears regularly on television, and his writing has been featured in the *Daily Wire*, the *Claremont Reviews of Books*, the *American Conservative*, the *American Mind*, and FOX News. Knowles is a graduate of Yale University and has lectured at universities and research institutes around the world.

CHAPTER 24

GROVER CLEVELAND

The Twenty-Second and Twenty-Fourth President

By Wilfred McClay

In 1881, Grover Cleveland was an obscure Buffalo, New York, attorney. In 1885, he was president of the United States.

No one in public life has ever risen higher faster.

He did it not by dint of a great fortune or great connections but by virtue of his virtue. He was a man of unassailable integrity—he did what he thought was right no matter the political cost.

In an era notorious for rampant corruption, Cleveland's integrity drove his fellow politicians crazy—and made him a hero to voters. The proof? He won the popular vote in three consecutive presidential elections—a feat accomplished by only two other presidents: Andrew Jackson and Franklin Roosevelt.

Cleveland also won the Electoral College vote in the first and third of those elections, making him the twenty-second and twenty-fourth president of the United States.

Born on March 18, 1837, in Caldwell, New Jersey, Cleveland was the fifth of nine children. His father was a minister from a line of ministers, stretching back at least four generations.

But Cleveland took up the law, where his indefatigable work habits and attention to detail served him well.

By his mid-twenties, he had established himself as a leading attorney in Buffalo.

He was a workaholic, and he seems to have had little interest in marriage or family. He preferred to spend his free time visiting Buffalo taverns for beer and bratwurst.

It was in one such tavern that his political career began. There, Cleveland was dragooned by local Democratic power brokers into running for city mayor—a privilege better-connected prospects had already turned down. The mayor's office was known to be a sinkhole of corruption. That, as it turned out, made it the right job for Cleveland.

In a matter of months, Cleveland took on the city's entrenched interests, canceling bad contracts and cutting wasteful spending.

Could Cleveland take his "clean up the city" act to the state level? Democratic Party leaders thought so. After only a year as Buffalo's mayor, he was the Democrats' candidate for governor of New York. Drawing voters from both parties, he won that election in a landslide.

He did for New York what he did for Buffalo: slashing budgets, vetoing pork barrel spending, and refusing to appoint machine lackeys to government positions.

What was left to conquer? Well, the Democrats hadn't won a presidential election since 1856—almost three decades. Could Cleveland get them back to the White House?

The answer was yes: just like the voters of New York, the American people wanted someone to clean up Washington. But first, he had to get elected, and that wouldn't be easy. The Republicans had uncovered a skeleton in Cleveland's closet: a plausible allegation that he had fathered a child out of wedlock in Buffalo.

True to character, Cleveland never denied it. And much to the Republicans' surprise, it actually strengthened Cleveland's reputation—he would not lie.

Cleveland won the 1884 election, but just barely.

Fifteen months into his term, at age forty nine, he finally took a wife, marrying the daughter of his late law partner—the only president to marry in the White House.

Cleveland governed with the same unyielding integrity he had shown in Buffalo and Albany. He issued 414 vetoes, many of them for spending that he deemed unnecessary.

His fealty to the law was almost absolute. When white settlers agitated to break a treaty with the Winnebago and Crow Creek tribes in the Dakota Territory, Cleveland said no.

Such principled positions, and the inflexible way he pursued them, did not help him when he ran for reelection in 1888. He failed to carry even his own state of New York, and lost to the Republican, Benjamin Harrison.

His wife, Frances, however, was confident they would return. She told the White House butler "Take good care of all the furniture. . . . We are coming back four years from today."

Four years later, in 1893, they did. The American people had missed Cleveland's dedication to limited and honest government.

His moment of vindication, however, didn't last long. When the railroad boom went bust and commodity prices collapsed, the Panic of 1893 was on. It was the worst economic depression in American history until the Great Depression of the 1930s.

The panic completely overwhelmed Cleveland's second term. His party believed that the way out of the crisis was to coin more silver, but Cleveland had always been a strong defender of the gold standard. He wasn't going to change now. By the time 1896 rolled around, Cleveland no longer represented the views of his own party—their loyalty had shifted to people like William Jennings Bryan, the leader of the pro-silver movement.

It was a sad ending to an admirable political career. He had been defeated twice, first by Harrison, and then by the economy.

And yet Cleveland is a sterling example of what principled and impartial dedication to public service looks like. Journalist H. L. Mencken, who rarely had a nice word to say about anyone, had a nice word for Cleveland: "He came into office his own man and he went out without yielding anything of that character. . . ."

How many politicians are remembered like that?

Wilfred McClay holds the Victor Davis Hanson Chair in Classical History and Western Civilization at Hillsdale College. Before coming to Hillsdale in the fall of 2021, he was the G. T. and Libby Blankenship Chair in the History of Liberty at the University of Oklahoma, and the director of the Center for the History of Liberty.

His book *The Masterless* received the 1995 Merle Curti Award of the Organization of American Historians. Among his other books are *The Student's Guide to U.S. History*, *Religion Returns to the Public Square*, and *Land of Hope*.

He served for eleven years on the National Council on the Humanities, the advisory board for the National Endowment for the Humanities, and is currently a member of the US Commission on the Semiquincentennial.

He is a graduate of St. John's College and received his Ph.D. in history from Johns Hopkins University.

CHAPTER 25

BENJAMIN HARRISON

One-Term Wonder

By Louis Picone

If anybody thinks of Benjamin Harrison—and very few people do—they think of him as the guy whose presidency is sandwiched between the two terms of Grover Cleveland.

But the twenty-third president of the United States is much more than the answer to a trivia question. One could make the case that Harrison was among the most consequential single-term presidents in American history.

Here's just a partial list of what he accomplished in four years:

- Pushed through the first serious legislation to protect consumers: the Meat Inspection Act.
- Promoted merit over patronage as the basis of government employment, appointing a young, brash reformer named Theodore Roosevelt to the Civil Service Commission.
- Added six western states to the Union—a presidential record: North Dakota, South Dakota, Montana, Washington, Idaho, and Wyoming.
- Designated 22 million acres as forest reserves, establishing Sequoia and Yosemite National Parks.
- Signed the Sherman Antitrust Act, enabling the federal government to break up monopolies.
- Made America a legitimate naval power by adding over two dozen steel ships to the fleet. And . . .
- Established Ellis Island, bringing order to the nation's immigration process.

There's a reason why Frederick Douglass, the great civil rights leader, said of Harrison, "We never had a greater president."

As much as any president in the second half of the nineteenth century, Harrison was repelled by the injustices inflicted on black Americans. He was committed to doing something about it.

"When and under what conditions is the black man to have a free ballot? When is he in fact to have those full civil rights which have so long been his in law?"

He answered the first question by endorsing legislation to protect blacks' right to vote. That right had been enshrined in the Fifteenth Amendment, but it was being subverted by the Democrat-dominated South.

Had he not been opposed by every Democrat and undermined by a few Republicans, the institutionalized racism of Jim Crow might have been a historical footnote rather than a terrible stain on America's history.

Cynics might say, since blacks voted almost 100 percent Republican, Harrison had every reason to push such legislation. But Harrison was more than a politician, he was a deeply moral person. His views on the treatment of black Americans were well established before he entered the White House.

No one came to that residence with a better pedigree than Harrison. His great-grandfather Benjamin Harrison V signed the Declaration of Independence. His grandfather William Henry Harrison was the ninth president of the United States, and his father, John Scott Harrison, served in the House of Representatives.

Benjamin Harrison was born on August 20, 1833, in North Bend, Ohio. Although always aware of his impressive lineage, he never used it to his own advantage. As he told an audience early in his career, "I want it understood, that I am the grandson of nobody. I believe that every man should stand on his own merits."

He attended Miami University in Ohio to be close to his future wife, Caroline Scott. After graduation, he and his new bride moved to Indianapolis, where Harrison practiced law.

With his strong antislavery leanings, he also joined the Republican Party almost as soon as it was formed.

Then in 1862, he left his now-prosperous legal career to enlist in the Union army.

Like future presidents Hayes, Garfield, and McKinley, he served with distinction, rising from colonel to brigadier general. He saw heavy action under General Sherman in the Atlanta campaign.

After the war, Harrison returned to the law, becoming one of the leading attorneys in Indiana. In 1881, he was elected to the US Senate.

Once again, he distinguished himself as a model public servant—honest, hardworking, and, in Harrison's case, a gifted orator. These qualities earned him serious consideration in the race for the 1888 Republican nomination for president.

Harrison wasn't anyone's first choice, but he was everyone's second choice. That proved good enough. He won the nomination in a field of seven candidates on the eighth ballot.

And then he beat the sitting Democratic president, Grover Cleveland. Harrison won by combining something old with something new. The "old" was high tariffs to protect American businesses from foreign competition—a Republican staple since Lincoln.

The "new" was generous pensions to Civil War veterans—a popular policy Cleveland strongly opposed.

It was a very close election. Cleveland won more votes, but Harrison won the Electoral College and, thus, the presidency.

Workmanlike in everything he did, Harrison's four years in office, as I've already described, were incredibly productive.

In 1892, Harrison was again opposed by Grover Cleveland. But this time, several factors worked against Harrison. The Civil War pensions busted the budget, consuming almost 40 percent of total spending, resulting in the first "Billion Dollar Congress." The high tariffs that had helped Harrison win in 1888 by protecting industry in the East alienated farmers and ranchers in the West.

No less damaging but much more tragic, his wife, Caroline, was dying of tuberculosis. Harrison refused to leave her side and never campaigned on his own behalf.

Two weeks before the election, she died.
So stricken with grief was Harrison, he barely noticed he had lost.

Louis Picone is the award-winning author of *Grant's Tomb: The Epic Death of Ulysses S. Grant and the Making of an American Pantheon*; *The President Is Dead! The Extraordinary Stories of the Presidential Deaths, Final Days, Burials, and Beyond*; and *Where the Presidents Were Born: The History & Preservation of the Presidential Birthplaces.*

Picone is a member of the Authors Guild, the American Historical Association, and the Ulysses S. Grant Monument Association, and is also a trustee on the board of the Grover Cleveland Birthplace Memorial Association. He holds a master's in history and teaches at William Paterson University.

Picone has spoken on the topic of presidential sites at the White House Historical Association Presidential Sites Summit, the James A. Garfield National Historic Site, and the Russian Academy of Sciences in Moscow. He has appeared on C-SPAN, the BBC, and NPR, and his writing has been published in *Time* and the *Washington Post.*

CHAPTER 26

WILLIAM McKINLEY

The Man Who Could've Been on Rushmore

By Jason R. Edwards

There are four presidents on Mount Rushmore: Washington, Jefferson, Lincoln, and Teddy Roosevelt. Were it not for a crazed assassin, the face of William McKinley—and not TR—very well could have been carved on that mountain.

As it stands, the twenty-fifth president of the United States is almost a historical afterthought.

That's a shame because, as much as anyone, McKinley laid the foundation for American dominance of the twentieth century.

William McKinley was born on January 29, 1843, in Niles, Ohio. As far back as anyone could remember, he was sober, cautious, and responsible. He adored his deeply religious, abolitionist mother. She wanted him to become a minister, but when the Civil War broke out, eighteen-year-old William joined the Union army as a private. He wrote his sister that he had decided "to serve my country in this, her perilous hour, from a sense of duty."

He quickly came to the attention of his commanding officer, fellow Ohioan and future president Rutherford B. Hayes, who made McKinley his chief quartermaster. As even-tempered as McKinley was, he was not afraid of taking great risks if he thought they were necessary. At the bloody Battle of Antietam, he drove a wagon full of food and water through heavy enemy fire to desperate Union soldiers.

"God bless the lad," wrote Officer James Comley of McKinley's heroic action.

Until the end of his life, McKinley preferred to be addressed by his final army rank—Major—saying, "I earned that. I am not so sure of the rest."

At age twenty-two, the veteran McKinley returned to Ohio, intent on a legal career. He quickly established himself as an extremely competent attorney.

In 1871, he married Ida Saxton, the daughter of a prominent local banker. They had two children, but both died tragically—one from typhoid fever at the age of three and one shortly after birth. These losses shattered Ida's physical and emotional health. McKinley remained devoted to his wife, often spending hours a day with her, even during the busiest times of his political career.

McKinley was elected to Congress in 1876 and served there until 1891, ultimately becoming the chairman of the powerful Ways and Means Committee. His defining issue was the tariff. Like most Republicans of that era, he believed that American industry and workers needed protection from cheap foreign labor to thrive. The 1890 "McKinley Tariff" cemented his thinking into law.

It was on this issue that McKinley wanted to run as the 1896 Republican nominee for president. But the deciding issue turned out to be gold vs. silver—specifically, on which metal would the currency be based. McKinley was a "sound money man"—that is, he favored gold, the long-established foundation of the global economy. His Democratic opponent, William Jennings Bryan, favored silver. Crisscrossing the nation, Bryan famously proclaimed that "You shall not crucify mankind upon a cross of gold!" McKinley, however, calmly remained on his front porch, winning the argument and the election.

Shortly after his presidency began, the gold issue faded, replaced by a brewing crisis ninety miles off the Florida coast: Cuban rebels were in full revolt against their Spanish overlords.

Reports of Spanish atrocities outraged the American people.

The popular press whipped this outrage into a frenzy. Demands for McKinley to intervene on the side of the Cuban freedom fighters were overwhelming.

But McKinley had seen war up close and knew its horrible reality.

Even when an explosion on February 15, 1898, destroyed the American battleship the USS *Maine* in Havana Harbor, killing over 250 sailors—the press insisting it was an act of Spanish aggression—McKinley held back. By this point, he was convinced that war was probably inevitable but was worried that the army and navy were not fully prepared.

Finally satisfied that America was ready, on April 25 he signed a declaration of war.

The Spanish-American War lasted less than four months, ending in an overwhelming American victory. There were 385 American battlefield deaths, roughly two thousand more dying from tropical disease.

The Spanish colonies of Cuba, Puerto Rico, Guam, and the Philippines came under American control. Hawaii, now more critical than ever as a naval station, was also annexed.

America had arrived as a global power, and everyone knew it.

That included most American voters. In 1900, McKinley easily won his reelection for a second term.

He came into his new term full of optimism. He had a strengthened majority in Congress and a vigorous, new vice president, the governor of New York, and hero of the recent war, Theodore Roosevelt.

McKinley had an ambitious agenda. Among his goals were securing the victories of the Spanish-American War, opening international markets for trade, particularly in China, augmenting civil rights for blacks, and finalizing negotiations to start building the Panama Canal.

And then fate intervened.

While attending the Pan-American Exposition in Buffalo, New York, on September 6, 1901, McKinley was shot by a self-proclaimed anarchist. He died eight days later.

Teddy Roosevelt took up McKinley's mantle. In doing so, the charismatic new president permanently overshadowed his predecessor on his way to Mount Rushmore.

Fair or unfair, that's how history frequently works.

Jason Edwards is a professor of history at Grove City College and a Fellow for Popular Culture with the Institute for Faith & Freedom. He has published writings on history, culture, and education in a variety of newspapers and journals, including the *Washington Times*, the *University Bookman*, and *Touchstone*.

Edwards has served on the board of the Society for Classical Learning and was also instrumental in developing the classical studies minor offered at Grove City College.

A former Lehrman Scholar and Salvatori Fellow with the Intercollegiate Studies Institute, Edwards's research interests center on agrarian philosophy and the history of learning in Western civilization. He coauthored the book *Ask the Professor: What Freshmen Need to Know.*

Edwards received his bachelor's degree from Asbury College and both his master's degree and doctorate from the University of Kentucky.

CHAPTER 27

THEODORE ROOSEVELT

City Slicker to Cowboy President

By Wilfred McClay

Now look, that damned cowboy is President of the United States!"

That was the reaction of Ohio Senator Mark Hanna, after learning that his close political ally, President William McKinley, had been assassinated.

"That damned cowboy" was Theodore Roosevelt.

Roosevelt had literally been a cowboy. He had also been a war hero, politician, historian, explorer, big-game hunter, ornithologist, and serious amateur boxer—and that's not even a complete list.

Now he was adding another job: twenty-sixth president of the United States.

Theodore Roosevelt was born in New York City on October 27, 1858, to a patrician family of Dutch heritage. Homeschooled for his entire youth, he benefited from tutors and widespread foreign travel. In 1876, he entered Harvard. When he wasn't editing the campus literary magazine, he was rowing, boxing, and participating in a half dozen Harvard social clubs.

But it would be a mistake to think that TR had an easy life. As a boy, he suffered from asthma, poor eyesight, chronic headaches, fevers, and stomach pains. But he overcame those disabilities with the determination that would become his trademark.

Eventually, he increased both his strength and stamina, which he showed off to others with an irrepressible boyish enthusiasm that charmed many and annoyed many.

Inspired by his father's civic-mindedness, he chose a career in politics. In 1881, he was elected to the New York State Assembly. Within a year—just twenty-four years old—he became his party's minority leader.

Then it all came crashing down.

Both his wife, Alice, and mother, Martha, died within hours of each other on, of all days, Valentine's Day 1884.

Grief-stricken, Roosevelt fled the concrete canyons of New York for the real canyons of the Dakota Territory. For two years, he distracted himself hunting buffalo, herding cattle, and writing about the American West. But he couldn't stay away from politics.

When he returned to the city in 1886, he resumed his steady rise through the ranks of New York and national politics, first as a member of the Civil Service Commission under President Benjamin Harrison, then as the New York City police commissioner, and then as assistant secretary of the navy under President William McKinley.

While in this position, TR pushed hard for America to take the side of the Cuban rebels in revolt against their Spanish colonial masters. When the Spanish-American War broke out in 1898, TR traded in his suit and tie for a military uniform.

His famous charge up San Juan Hill made him a national hero.

Armed with this new reputation, he was elected governor of New York in 1898. He immediately clashed with New York Republican Party boss Thomas Platt. So anxious was Platt to get the independent-minded governor out of New York politics that he arranged for Roosevelt to become McKinley's running mate in the 1900 presidential election.

As vice president, Roosevelt nearly went crazy from boredom. McKinley, like most chief executives, gave his vice president almost nothing to do.

And then on September 6, 1901, McKinley was shot by a mentally disturbed anarchist in Buffalo, New York. Eight days later, he succumbed to his wounds. Theodore Roosevelt, the cowboy, was now president—at forty-two, the youngest man ever to occupy the office.

While he promised to fulfill McKinley's agenda—and for the most part he did—Roosevelt was his own man with his own distinctive governing philosophy.

TR believed that the president should set the legislative agenda for Congress, not the other way around—which had been the norm for most of American history.

He was also not particularly deferential to the Constitution, which limits executive power. TR argued that a president was permitted to do anything that was not expressly forbidden by the Constitution.

For example, when coal miners went on strike in May 1902, Roosevelt threatened to send the army to operate the mines. Asked whether that would be constitutional, Roosevelt replied, "To hell with the Constitution when the people want coal!"

Roosevelt applied the same assertiveness to foreign policy as, for example, in the creation of the Panama Canal. When the Colombian government refused to lease the US the isthmus of Panama, Roosevelt took matters into his own hands.

He told his secretary of state, John Hay, "I do not think that the Bogota lot of jackrabbits should be allowed permanently to bar one of the future highways of civilization."

TR sent a fleet of American warships to the Colombian coast to aid the nascent Panamanian separatist movement. When the rebels declared their independence from Colombia, Roosevelt immediately recognized the new country of Panama and made a favorable deal for the canal.

His critics shouted "Imperialism!," but most Americans were thrilled. As a new century dawned, the nation was on the move and nobody moved more decisively than Roosevelt. That "damned cowboy" had arrived, and, it seemed, so had America.

Wilfred McClay holds the Victor Davis Hanson Chair in Classical History and Western Civilization at Hillsdale College. Before coming to Hillsdale in the fall of 2021, he was the G. T. and Libby Blankenship Chair in the History of Liberty at the University of Oklahoma, and the director of the Center for the History of Liberty.

His book *The Masterless* received the 1995 Merle Curti Award of the Organization of American Historians. Among his other books are *The Student's Guide to U.S. History*, *Religion Returns to the Public Square*, and *Land of Hope*.

He served for eleven years on the National Council on the Humanities, the advisory board for the National Endowment for the Humanities, and is currently a member of the US Commission on the Semiquincentennial.

He is a graduate of St. John's College and received his Ph.D. in history from Johns Hopkins University.

CHAPTER 28

THEODORE ROOSEVELT

The Action Hero President

By Wilfred McClay

Even the Democrats knew that beating Theodore Roosevelt in the presidential election of 1904 was a long shot.

They were right.

TR was still the hero of the Spanish-American War; still the personification of energetic, forward-looking America.

He had just had a very successful three and a half years. He fulfilled much of his late predecessor's agenda—advancing the Panama Canal project, for example—while realizing his own ambitions in his own unique way: like going after the big corporate monopolies.

Indeed, the election was a total wipeout. TR won with a bigger margin of victory than anyone since James Monroe—who ran unopposed—and that was in 1820.

With four more years ahead of him, it seemed like there was nothing Roosevelt couldn't accomplish. He hit the ground running, pushing through new railroad regulations and consumer protections, such as the Pure Food and Drug Act.

Conservation of natural resources was of special interest. Roosevelt was an outdoorsman, and his experiences in the Dakotas gave him a keen appreciation of the open spaces of the American West. He wanted them preserved.

He established the Forest Service, signed into law the creation of five national parks, and proclaimed eighteen new national monuments. The total area he placed under public protection was approximately 230 million acres.

And he didn't confine himself to domestic concerns. America had become the number one economy in the world. Now, Teddy believed, it had to become the greatest military power in the world. To make his point, Roosevelt sent the new American naval fleet on a worldwide tour from 1907 to 1909. The "Great White Fleet" as it was called, personified Teddy's famous line, "Speak softly and carry a big stick."

Back home, however, there was nothing soft about his speech, especially when it came to those opposing his policies. He denounced the "malefactors of great wealth" for their "predatory" behavior. To counteract them, he signed a bill restricting corporations from making political contributions. He also pushed for federal control over the stock market and called for a permanent income tax.

Such proposals and such rhetoric antagonized the conservative "Old Guard" of the Republican Party. Even though they managed to block portions of Roosevelt's agenda, they couldn't block his reforming zeal. The people were with him—that's what mattered.

He used that popularity to promote his hand-picked successor, Secretary of War William Howard Taft. The choice was an odd one, given that Roosevelt had such an expansive view of the powers of the presidency while Taft believed the opposite—that the president was restrained by the letter of the Constitution.

After Taft won an easy victory in the 1908 presidential election, Teddy vowed to stay out of politics. After the inauguration, he embarked on a yearlong hunting trip to Africa, followed by a highly successful tour of Europe, where he was feted by virtually every head of state.

Even while he was gone, though, he was losing faith in the more conservative and cautious Taft. Roosevelt felt that Taft was squandering his legacy, and that was something he simply couldn't abide.

The differences between the two men exploded into a one-sided feud. Taft wanted peace, but Teddy was spoiling for a fight. The rift deeply wounded Taft, who lamented, "Roosevelt was my closest friend."

By now, TR was a full-on Progressive, advocating for an early form of Social Security, for weakening of property rights, and even for allowing voters to overturn unpopular judicial decisions. Taft was alarmed. These proposals envisioned a government and a chief executive far beyond anything the Founders had intended.

It soon became clear that this was not just a personal squabble between mentor and mentee. The showdown came in Chicago at the Republican Convention in the summer of 1912. Roosevelt had the crowd, but Taft had the party.

After Roosevelt failed to get the nomination, he and the party's Progressive wing stormed out of the Chicago Coliseum and formed a new party, the Progressive or, as Teddy called it, "Bull-Moose" Party.

"We stand at Armageddon and we battle for the Lord!" he thundered at the party's impromptu convention.

He threw himself into his third-party campaign with his usual unrestrained vigor.

Even an assassination attempt in which he was seriously wounded couldn't silence him. In fact, it didn't even stop him from giving a speech that same day.

When the results were in, it was the most successful third-party run in American history, garnering more votes, popular and electoral alike, than the Republican Party. But ultimately, it split the Republican vote and handed the election to the little-known Democrat, Woodrow Wilson, a man who would push the country in a new, leftward direction far beyond that envisioned by Roosevelt, let alone Taft.

That was the dark side of TR. His boldness could veer into overconfidence—even narcissism. Others would have to pay the consequences.

But we must not forget the brighter side: the indomitable, idealistic, action-hero president who, more than almost anyone else, represents the American spirit of adventure and possibility.

Wilfred McClay holds the Victor Davis Hanson Chair in Classical History and Western Civilization at Hillsdale College. Before coming to Hillsdale in the fall of 2021, he was the G. T. and Libby Blankenship Chair in the History of Liberty at the University of Oklahoma, and the director of the Center for the History of Liberty.

His book *The Masterless* received the 1995 Merle Curti Award of the Organization of American Historians. Among his other books are *The Student's Guide to U.S. History*, *Religion Returns to the Public Square*, and *Land of Hope*.

He served for eleven years on the National Council on the Humanities, the advisory board for the National Endowment for the Humanities, and is currently a member of the US Commission on the Semiquincentennial.

He is a graduate of St. John's College and received his Ph.D. in history from Johns Hopkins University.

CHAPTER 29

WILLIAM HOWARD TAFT

The Really Big President

By Richard Lim

You could argue that the two most powerful figures in America are the president and the chief justice of the Supreme Court.

Only one man has been both: William Howard Taft.

Unfortunately, our twenty-seventh president and tenth chief justice is mostly remembered for being . . . well, fat.

And that's a shame because the focus on his weight has obscured a career that was as impressive as it was singular.

Taft was born in Cincinnati, Ohio, on September 15, 1857. There was never any doubt that William would become an attorney. His grandfather, Peter Taft, was a prominent lawyer in Vermont and his father, Alphonso Taft, served as attorney general under President Ulysses S. Grant.

To his father's endless frustration, young William was a notorious procrastinator—a trait that lasted a lifetime. He would wait until the last minute to prepare his schoolwork and, later on, his law cases. But that's all the time he needed, because when it counted, he was always prepared.

In 1880, after graduating from Yale, Taft took a degree in law. With some help from his father, he got a job as an assistant prosecutor in Cincinnati.

He rose quickly to become a judge in 1887. He was only twenty-nine.

In 1890, President Benjamin Harrison appointed him as America's solicitor general—serving in effect as the government's lead attorney. Taft thrived in the position, winning fifteen out of eighteen cases before the US Supreme Court.

In 1892, he returned to Cincinnati as a federal judge.

His ultimate ambition, a seat on the High Court, seemed to be within his grasp. When President William McKinley summoned him to the White House in 1900, Taft thought his dream might be coming true. But McKinley had another job for him: governor of the Philippines.

The United States had just acquired the islands as a prize of the Spanish-American War but didn't exactly know what to do with it. There were two problems: a lingering insurgency and no history of democracy.

The US military solved the first, and Taft solved the second.

He did it by patiently building up the islands' legal and physical infrastructure. More importantly, he did it by treating the Filipinos as equals, involving them in every step of the process.

No one ever doubted Taft's skills as a legal theorist—now they learned he was also a skilled administrator. His future secretary of war, Henry Stimson, who also served under presidents Herbert Hoover, Franklin Roosevelt, and Harry Truman, said Taft was the best administrator of them all.

The Filipino people so admired the work he had done on their behalf that when new President Theodore Roosevelt offered Taft a seat on the Supreme Court in 1903, they staged large public rallies to convince him to stay.

It worked—Taft turned down Roosevelt's offer.

Roosevelt finally got Taft back to the US, appointing him as secretary of war in 1904. Upon his return, Taft quickly won over his boss. Roosevelt gushed, "He has the most lovable personality I have ever come in contact with."

In 1908, Roosevelt declared Taft to be his preferred successor.

With TR's endorsement, Taft easily defeated Democratic candidate William Jennings Bryan.

As president, Taft continued many of Roosevelt's policies, such as busting trusts, regulating the railroad industry, and putting land under federal protection. In fact, Taft ended up busting more trusts and protecting more land than his fabled predecessor. He was also the first president to appoint a woman, Julia Lathrop, to head a federal agency, the US Children's Bureau.

One would think that Roosevelt would have been proud of his successor's record, but the two men diverged on a key issue: Taft was a constitutionalist. If he didn't believe a law or executive action was constitutional, he wouldn't do it. Teddy never cared much for such legal niceties. If he wanted to do something, he'd find a way around the Constitution.

This might have remained a philosophical dispute between friends, but it boiled over into open warfare when Roosevelt decided he wanted his old job back. When he failed to unseat his protégé at the 1912 Republican Convention, TR bolted the party altogether and ran as a third-party candidate.

Troubled by the burdens of the office and his rift with his old friend, Taft began to eat compulsively. His weight ballooned to 350 pounds. But no, the legend that he got stuck in a bathtub is not true.

Roosevelt and Democratic candidate Woodrow Wilson campaigned as Progressives, seeking to fundamentally change the American political system. Taft steered a more traditional course.

Unfortunately, his campaign theme—defending the Constitution—excited few voters at a time when progressivism was all the rage.

Roosevelt's candidacy split the Republican vote, handing the election to Wilson.

After leaving the White House, Taft served as a law professor at Yale. Freed from the stress of elective office, he promptly lost seventy-five pounds.

In 1921, Taft finally realized his life's ambition when Republican President Warren G. Harding appointed him as the chief justice of the Supreme Court.

As chief, Taft did more than any chief justice to modernize the court and secure its status as a coequal and independent branch of government.

This was best illustrated by Taft's push for the court to have its own building. For decades, it had met in the Capitol—symbolizing its dependence on Congress. Thanks to Taft, when the Supreme Court Building was completed in 1935, it finally had a structure worthy of its stature.

As far as Taft's own stature, we can say this: he was no lightweight.

Richard Lim is the cofounder and host of the *This American President* podcast. The success of his podcast landed him interviews with several prominent guests, including former CIA and NSA Director Michael Hayden, Apollo 13 astronaut Fred Haise, Secret Service Agent Clint Hill, and FOX News host Bret Baier.

Lim has previously served at the White House, the Association of the US Army, and George Washington's Mount Vernon estate. He regularly appears on the nationally syndicated radio show *Point of View's Millennial Round Table.*

Lim's opinion editorials have appeared in the Daily Signal, the *Washington Examiner*, RealClearHistory, and the History News Network. Mr. Lim obtained a master's degree in public administration from Syracuse University's Maxwell School and a bachelor's degree from the University of California, San Diego.

CHAPTER 30

WOODROW WILSON

The Founder of Big Government

By RJ Pestritto

Few American leaders have stirred more controversy than Woodrow Wilson, the twenty-eighth president of the United States. Many admire him; many don't. But one point on which everyone agrees is his profound impact on American history.

The reasons for the controversy and the impact are one and the same.

Wilson and his generation of leaders were the first to challenge the founding principles of the country. It's not an exaggeration to say that Wilson turned them upside down.

As expressed in the Declaration of Independence, the Founders believed that individuals are born with certain unalienable rights. And they framed the Constitution to protect those rights.

For Wilson, the time of individual rights had passed. In his view, eighteenth-century America had little relevance to early-twentieth-century America. The country, now much bigger and more complex, required the guidance of a benevolent government.

America had literally outgrown the Founders.

Wilson's philosophy—of which he was a leading proponent—was known as progressivism. And Wilson proudly called himself a Progressive.

Where did Wilson get these ideas? From the place where he spent most of his life: the halls of academia. He was the only US president to come into office with a Ph.D.

Born in Staunton, Virginia, on December 28, 1856, Woodrow Wilson had two ambitions: to teach and to write. He received his undergraduate degree from Princeton with the vague notion that he would become a lawyer. But like another, earlier president, John Quincy Adams, Wilson found the law much too arid for his active mind. To the chagrin of his father, he returned to academia to get an advanced degree at Johns Hopkins.

There, his thinking took form. He was deeply influenced by Charles Darwin's new theory of evolution. At Hopkins this theory was applied to government: just as a species must adapt—or progress—to survive, so must a government. Not to recognize this would be to hold America back, to stunt its growth, or, to close the metaphor, risk extinction.

This was one of the major themes in Wilson's Ph.D. thesis, which he turned into an influential book titled *Congressional Government: A Study in American Politics*. This book launched his academic career, which culminated in his appointment as president of Princeton in 1902.

As happy as he was at Princeton, Wilson longed to put his Progressive ideas to the test, hence his move into politics. There, his rise was truly meteoric. In 1910, he ran successfully for governor of New Jersey as a Democrat. Once in office, he surprised everyone with his impressive political skills, scoring one policy victory after another, while also fighting New Jersey's notoriously corrupt political machine.

Reforming workers' compensation, limiting how much money corporations could spend on elections, and putting utilities under state supervision were only three of the Progressive ideas he pushed through the legislature. His success attracted the attention of Progressives nationwide. In 1912, the Democratic Party, desperate to end a sixteen-year losing streak, turned to Wilson as its nominee.

The chances of Wilson winning that election against a united Republican Party were slim, but the electoral calculus changed dramatically when former Republican president Teddy Roosevelt decided to run against his own hand-picked successor, the current Republican president, William Taft.

TR's campaign was the most successful third-party run in American history, but all it accomplished was to split the Republicans and give Wilson an easy victory. He won with 42 percent of the popular vote, the lowest percentage since Lincoln.

In just three years, Wilson had risen from president of Princeton to president of the United States.

As he did as governor, he immediately went to work.

Wilson made the new income tax, only recently ratified by the Sixteenth Amendment, the most important source of government revenue. He put the nation's banking system under federal control by establishing the federal reserve system, and strengthened regulations to rein in private business.

But more than specific legislative wins, Wilson's program marked the arrival of the idea that government was not merely the servant of the people, but its savior. Ironically, he entitled his program, "The New Freedom."

Unfortunately, this didn't apply to black Americans. If anything, they saw their freedoms curtailed during Wilson's presidency. Unsympathetic to blacks' civil rights concerns, he resegregated the federal government, which previous Republican administrations had worked to integrate.

On the other hand, he did appoint the first Jewish Supreme Court justice, Louis Brandeis, one of the few people from whom Wilson would actually take advice.

Like all effective leaders, Wilson had a clear vision of what he wanted to accomplish: to reshape Americans' view of government. And in that, he ultimately succeeded.

His second term would present a whole new set of challenges. A terrible storm was brewing in Europe. It would give Wilson an opportunity not only to further change America but to change the world.

Ronald Pestritto is a Senior Fellow of the Claremont Institute and graduate dean and professor of politics at Hillsdale College, where he holds the Charles and Lucia Shipley Chair in the American Constitution.

Pestritto has published seven books, including *Woodrow Wilson and the Roots of Modern Liberalism* and *American Progressivism: A Reader.* His other books include an edited collection of Wilson's speeches and writings, *Woodrow Wilson: The Essential Political Writings*, and *Founding the Criminal Law: Punishment and Political Thought in the Origins of America.*

In addition to his academic work, Pestritto has written widely on progressivism and the administrative state.

Pestritto earned his B.A. from Claremont McKenna College and his Ph.D. from the Claremont Graduate University.

CHAPTER 31

WOODROW WILSON

World War I and the League of Nations

By RJ Pestritto

For over a hundred years, the United States of America had relied on the genius of individuals to solve problems. It was often chaotic but incredibly productive, leading to the greatest economic expansion in world history.

For Woodrow Wilson, the twenty-eighth president of the United States, the time had come to bring order to that chaos. That would mean less freedom for the individual, but, at least in theory, more equality across society.

It was an exchange that perfectly fit into his Progressive worldview: that the government should be active in every aspect of American life.

In a remarkable first term, Wilson laid the groundwork for this transformation of America.

In his second term, Wilson sought to transform the world.

The First World War—1914 to 1918—gave him the opportunity.

Initially, Wilson did everything he could to keep the nation out of that war. In fact, the reason he won his reelection in 1916 was his promise not to send American boys to fight on another continent.

But within two years, over 2 million Americans would be on that continent. Over a hundred thousand would die.

German aggression, specifically its submarine warfare that killed hundreds of Americans, made it very difficult for Wilson to keep the nation out of the war.

The final straw was the infamous "Zimmermann Telegram" in which the German government promised to help Mexico reclaim much of the Southwest if Mexico would stir up trouble along the Rio Grande.

On April 2, 1917, Wilson asked for a declaration of war. Congress gave it to him four days later.

If Wilson believed the government was supreme during peacetime, how much more so during wartime? To supercharge the war effort, Wilson essentially took control of the US economy. He nationalized whole industries, rationed food and fuel, fixed prices, and raised the top income tax rate to 77 percent.

Civil liberties were severely curtailed. Criticism of the war was essentially forbidden. Violators were imprisoned under the Espionage and Sedition Acts of 1917 and 1918. German composers like Bach and Beethoven were banned, teaching the German language in schools was prohibited, and sauerkraut was renamed "liberty cabbage."

To his credit, Wilson left the prosecution of the war to his generals, and America did indeed turn the tide in favor of the Allies.

On November 11, 1918, the Germans, unable to counter America's economic and military might, agreed to stop fighting.

Peace was at hand.

But what would that peace look like?

As always, Wilson had a vision. He called it the "Fourteen Points."

The key point was the creation of an international League of Nations.

Wilson was so committed to this idea that he decided to go to Europe personally and negotiate the peace agreement. Europeans greeted him as a conquering hero, lining the streets wherever he went.

Wilson's impulse was to give Germany generous peace terms. He wanted what he called "peace without victory." But the French and British saw things much differently. Having suffered so grievously, they wanted Germany severely punished.

Wilson thought that was a terrible mistake but eventually yielded. It was a price he was willing to pay to get the Allies to agree to his League of Nations.

But while Wilson had sold the league to the Europeans, he couldn't sell it to Congress.

Republicans and even some Democrats were leery that the league required member nations to counter "external aggression" against "all members." They feared this could lead to endless American involvement in foreign wars.

Wilson brushed aside their concerns and took his case directly to the American people, convinced that once they understood it, they would embrace it. The speaking tour took everything Wilson had and more.

On October 2, 1919, he suffered a massive stroke, rendering him partially paralyzed.

Amazingly, his medical condition was concealed from the American public—and even from his own cabinet—during the final eighteen months of his presidency.

In this unprecedented situation, his wife, Edith, secretly issued directives on her husband's behalf. Some have called her America's first female president.

Had Wilson been willing to compromise with Senate Republicans on the league question, maybe he could have gotten it ratified. But he refused.

In a stinging rebuke, the Senate rejected Wilson's dream. One year later the American people pronounced their own verdict. They elected Republican Warren Harding to be their new president in a landslide.

They had had enough of Wilson's progressivism. But the setback was only temporary. The ideas that Wilson espoused—government entry into many aspects of our lives and, with it, the massive expansion of the federal bureaucracy—would be given new life with the ascension of another Democrat and Wilson protégé, Franklin Roosevelt.

Wilson's big government ideas are still with us today. They are his true and lasting legacy.

⁘

Ronald Pestritto is a Senior Fellow of the Claremont Institute and graduate dean and professor of politics at Hillsdale College, where he holds the Charles and Lucia Shipley Chair in the American Constitution.

Pestritto has published seven books, including *Woodrow Wilson and the Roots of Modern Liberalism* and *American Progressivism: A Reader*. His other books include an edited collection of Wilson's speeches and writings, *Woodrow Wilson: The Essential Political Writings*, and *Founding the Criminal Law: Punishment and Political Thought in the Origins of America*.

In addition to his academic work, Pestritto has written widely on progressivism and the administrative state.

Pestritto earned his B.A. from Claremont McKenna College and his Ph.D. from the Claremont Graduate University.

CHAPTER 32

WARREN HARDING

The Least-Appreciated President

By Amity Shlaes

Sometimes a president who appears pathetic is actually just plain tragic. And because he is a president, his tragedy is also the nation's.

That was the case of Warren Harding, the twenty-ninth president of the United States.

Harding was perhaps the most misunderstood and least appreciated of all America's chief executives.

Born in 1865 in a small Ohio town halfway between Cleveland and Columbus, Harding was a brave and unusual politician.

He didn't start as a politician. He spent most of his life as the editor and publisher of an Ohio newspaper, the *Marion Star*. Harding ran unsuccessfully for governor in 1910 and then successfully for senator in 1914.

In the presidential election year of 1920, Harding was considered a dark horse at best, but he emerged after ten ballots as the Republicans' choice. He certainly looked and even acted the part. Tall, with thick white hair and deep, penetrating eyes, Harding was as genial as he was handsome. To know him was to like him.

And Americans did like him. He won the 1920 election in a landslide, garnering an astonishing 60 percent of the popular vote.

The country that Warren Harding and his running mate Calvin Coolidge inherited faced multiple crises.

To win World War I, the government had taken over large sectors of the economy.

But what works in war doesn't always work in peace.

There was an inflation crisis: Prices for basic necessities like milk and butter rose at alarming rates. Prices that businesses paid for materials doubled.

There was a tax crisis: Corporate taxes were so heavy that businesses couldn't expand.

There was a labor crisis: Tens of thousands of Americans, many disabled, returned from Europe to find a stagnant economy short of jobs.

Angry workers mounted violent strikes.

And there was a government debt crisis, a result of war spending.

By 1920, it seemed that life in crisis was the new normal.

Absolutely not, said Harding.

Harding vowed to end the war laws and rules, to let the country go back to the way things were before the war.

He wanted commonsense life, the kind that had enabled Henry Ford to start his auto business.

"America's present need," Harding said, "is not heroics, but healing; not nostrums, but normalcy. . . ."

"Normalcy" was the motto Harding and Coolidge gave their campaign.

The Harding plans for normalcy were simple:

Let the Federal Reserve tighten money to wring inflation out of the economy.

Cut spending so that the government can pay off the war debt.

Cut tax rates to free business and encourage hiring.

Block new entitlement payments, even to veterans. Instead, build veterans hospitals.

Return those industries that wartime government had taken over back to private hands.

In short, give the economy and individuals the freedom to find their own way.

After taking office, Harding made all the right moves. He named a tough cabinet, including the nation's great master of debt, the banker Andrew Mellon, to the treasury post.

Harding coaxed Congress into giving the president the executive power he needed to analyze and stop excess spending through the Budget and Accounting Act of 1921.

Finally, Harding pushed through tax cuts for individuals and businesses. And for the veterans he funded special hospitals, the origin of Veterans Affairs.

All the pieces were in place for a return to the old normal that Harding had promised.

For the first time in a while, America's future looked bright.

But here is Harding's tragedy: the man lacked discipline. He planned well but executed poorly.

For example, when it came to those hospitals for veterans, the men Harding put in charge of construction took kickbacks and did shoddy work.

When it came to the promised privatization of government oil reserves, Harding looked away when friends leased reserves to their friends. The scandal would be known as Teapot Dome.

Harding besmirched the very principles he was advancing.

The pressure on Harding kept mounting. He could handle attacks from his enemies, he told a journalist. It was his friends, his "damn friends," who kept him awake at night.

In the summer of 1923, Harding traveled west. While at the Palace Hotel in San Francisco, Harding passed away suddenly—doubtless due to the pressure of mounting scandal. The new president, Calvin Coolidge, was left to clean up.

In the years that followed the country rose again—in part because Coolidge marshaled the discipline Harding lacked.

But also because of those Harding policies with the quirky name, normalcy.

Yet Harding was not around to see his own success. Over the decades salacious stories about his scandals obscured his impressive achievements.

That's Harding's real tragedy. And our own.

Amity Shlaes is the acclaimed author of several *New York Times* bestsellers, including *The Forgotten Man: A New History of the Great Depression*, *Coolidge*, and *The Greedy Hand: How Taxes Drive Americans Crazy*. She is also the author of *Great Society: A New History*, a comprehensive account of the Johnson administration's most notable legacy.

Shlaes chairs the board of the Calvin Coolidge Presidential Foundation, a national foundation based at the birthplace of President Coolidge. The foundation's goal is to share Coolidge with Americans, by hosting debate and events at the Coolidge site and through newer media.

She has been a syndicated columnist for more than a decade. Her pieces have appeared in *National Review*, *Forbes*, Bloomberg News, the *Wall Street Journal*, *Foreign Affairs*, and the *American Spectator*.

Shlaes is a graduate of Yale College.

CHAPTER 33

CALVIN COOLIDGE

The Best President You Don't Know

By Amity Shlaes

Do more.

That's what Americans demand of their presidents these days. A real president, Democrat or Republican, knows how to use "the office." A real president makes things happen. Or so goes the conventional wisdom.

But actually, there is another model. A president can succeed through inaction, by doing as little as possible. One such president was Calvin Coolidge, who took office upon Warren Harding's sudden death. From the time Coolidge became president in 1923 to the time he left in 1929, Coolidge served a philosophy that was simple and powerful: don't do.

Coolidge was our great refrainer.

The leadership style matched the personal style. Coolidge did not waste words. Hence his nickname, Silent Cal.

For these quiet ways, the thirtieth president absorbed much abuse. A Washington socialite, Alice Longworth, said that Coolidge looked like he had been weaned on a pickle.

Coolidge indeed cut a sharp contrast to Alice's father, Theodore Roosevelt, who had served a decade and a half earlier. And what a contrast Coolidge provides with another Roosevelt, Franklin, who came just a few years later.

Born on July 4, 1872, in rural Vermont, Coolidge embodied the simple virtues of his forebears. He was hardworking, sober, and cautious. He was also fearless. A lifelong civil servant, he worked his way up from city councilman to governor of Massachusetts. He made his political reputation by facing down the Boston Police Department when it went on strike in 1919. "There is no right to strike against the public safety by anybody, anywhere, any time," Coolidge told strikers. Then the Coolidge administration fired them all and built a new department from scratch. This made him a national hero—a politician with a backbone.

The refrainer brought that backbone into the White House and got the kind of results men of action long for.

Especially economic results. Low unemployment, often well below 5 percent. Low taxes. Higher wages. Fewer strikes. New technology for the masses—a Model A, or a Bell telephone, or an RCA radio.

And most remarkable of all, a shrinking federal budget. If you remember just one fact about Coolidge's presidency, let it be this: Coolidge left the federal budget lower than he found it.

How did Coolidge do it? First, he resisted taking unnecessary action himself. Second, he imposed the same discipline on Congress. That wasn't easy.

In the early 1920s, the Progressive movement was on the march. Just as now, Progressives always wanted to do something.

Progressive plans included more aid for agriculture, encouraging unions, increasing taxes, and nationalizing important industries, such as railroads and utilities.

Coolidge blocked the Progressives, and thereby blocked their expansion of government.

He vetoed farm subsidies twice, even though he personally came from farming country.

Coolidge was sympathetic to farmers, but helping them wasn't the government's function.

Coolidge made especially good use of the pocket veto, the ability of the president to veto a bill by simply not returning it to Congress. "It is much more important to kill a bad bill," he said, "than to pass a good one."

The legislation Coolidge did endorse was designed to meet the same minimalist end: restrain the government. Together with his treasury secretary, Andrew Mellon, Coolidge lowered the top tax rate to 25 percent. Their goal was to shrink the public sector, so that the private sector could expand. And the policy worked.

The country liked Coolidge's thrift. In the 1924 election, the Progressives won 17 percent of the vote. But Coolidge won with more votes than the Democrats and Progressives combined. So everyone, including his own Republican Party, thought Coolidge would surely run a second time in 1928. But he declined. Like George Washington, he thought the country needed a change in leaders.

Yes, it's possible to criticize Coolidge. As much as he tried to avoid it, Coolidge in the end signed bills he would have preferred not to. And the president showed a penchant for protectionism, rarely a sound economic policy. Some suggest that Coolidge was responsible for the stock market crash and the decade-long depression that followed after he left office.

But that's a fallacy. The Depression stretched so long not because of too little action from Calvin Coolidge, but because of too much action by his successors.

It is ironic that a man of such personal modesty presided over the era known as the Roaring Twenties.

But that was the paradox: Coolidge was a scrooge who begat plenty.

Perhaps, the day has come for a new politician to follow the great refrainer's rule. Where others do, don't. And if you have to do, do less.

Amity Shlaes is the acclaimed author of several *New York Times* bestsellers, including *The Forgotten Man: A New History of the Great Depression*, *Coolidge*, and *The Greedy Hand: How Taxes Drive Americans Crazy*. She is also the author of *Great Society: A New History*, a comprehensive account of the Johnson administration's most notable legacy.

Shlaes chairs the board of the Calvin Coolidge Presidential Foundation, a national foundation based at the birthplace of President Coolidge. The foundation's goal is to share Coolidge with Americans, by hosting debate and events at the Coolidge site and through newer media.

She has been a syndicated columnist for more than a decade. Her pieces have appeared in *National Review*, *Forbes*, Bloomberg News, the *Wall Street Journal*, *Foreign Affairs*, and the *American Spectator*.

Shlaes is a graduate of Yale College.

CHAPTER 34

HERBERT HOOVER

Success or Failure?

By Kenneth Whyte

Herbert Hoover, the thirty-first president of the United States, succeeded at almost everything he did.

And not just succeeded. He succeeded in spectacular fashion—as a mining executive in Australia and China, as a humanitarian in Europe, and as a politician in the United States.

But he is best known to history for his role in one failure—the Great Depression, a decade-long economic collapse that impoverished millions in America and across the world.

He didn't cause it. And he made superhuman efforts to reverse it. But no matter how hard he tried, he couldn't stop it.

If a single individual could have, it might have been this remarkable man.

Born in Iowa in 1874, he was orphaned at the age of nine. His father, a blacksmith, died when Hoover was just six; his mother, a Quaker preacher, three years later. Unhappy, sullen, and painfully shy as a teenager, he came into his own at Stanford University, then tuition-free. Hoover was in the university's very first graduating class, his field of study being geology.

On graduation, he talked himself into a job with a prominent English mining company. They sent him to the Australian outback. Conditions were so harsh, and disease so rampant, it was almost a suicide mission. But young Hoover was not deterred. He reorganized the company's mines, made them much more profitable, and scouted for new ones. A gold mine he acquired, largely on his own initiative, turned out to be one of the richest in the world.

He was on track to become fabulously wealthy when World War I broke out and he abruptly abandoned his business career.

In a matter of months, he transformed himself into an internationally recognized humanitarian. Almost single-handedly, he arranged to feed 8 million Belgians threatened with starvation when the war cut off their food supplies.

In 1919, with the guns finally silenced, Hoover was charged by President Woodrow Wilson to lead the rebuild of Europe's devastated economy. He tackled the job with usual ferocious energy and saved tens of millions more from starvation. The *New York Times* described him as "the nearest approach to a dictator Europe has had since Napoleon." They meant it as a compliment.

In 1921, the newly elected Republican president, Warren Harding, tapped Hoover to be secretary of commerce. He stayed on when Calvin Coolidge took over following Harding's sudden death in 1923. During his tenure, Hoover laid the groundwork for America's commercial aviation industry. He also organized the building of the Colorado River dam that now bears his name and made possible the rapid economic development of the American Southwest. And when disastrous flooding struck the Mississippi River Valley in 1927, it was Hoover who managed the massive and successful relief effort.

By the time he won the Republican presidential nomination in 1928, he was hailed as a man "whose wisdom encompassed all branches, whose judgment was never at fault, who knew the answers to all questions, and who could see in the dark." His election was never in doubt. He won easily.

Yet just six months after Hoover's inauguration, in the autumn of 1929, the stock market crashed. Slowly and inexorably, the United States followed the rest of the world into the Great Depression. However qualified he was for the presidency, Hoover was no match for the worst economic collapse in modern history, an international phenomenon rooted in the still-unresolved upheavals of the First World War, and far beyond the capacities of any one leader to solve.

His political opponents would later claim that he sat on his hands through his four years in office. Hoover, in fact, fought the Depression with vigor and imagination. He expanded the federal government's tool kit for managing the economy and made far more progress in limiting the Depression's damage than is generally recognized.

But the Depression exposed Hoover's weaknesses as a political leader. Always a workhorse, often brusque and even surly, he had succeeded in politics not because of his personality but in spite of it.

He made himself an easy target for Franklin Roosevelt, his Democratic challenger in 1932. A master of the political arts, Roosevelt effectively accused Hoover of not caring about the plight of millions of unemployed Americans. Hoover lacked the skills to counter Roosevelt's nonstop attacks. The charges stuck.

But it was his stance on Prohibition that really did Hoover in. Roosevelt strongly favored repeal. Hoover thought it should remain the law of the land.

Roosevelt won in a landslide.

An inveterate cigar smoker, the man from Stanford lived on for thirty more years, writing books, managing charities, and overseeing the conservative think tank that he founded and that still operates today.

Despite all he accomplished, Herbert Hoover is best remembered for his one great failure. We would do his memory and American history a service if we also remembered him for his astonishing successes.

Kenneth Whyte is a Canadian journalist, publisher, and author based in Toronto. He is currently the writer, owner, and publisher of Sutherland House press, and chairman of the Donner Canadian Foundation. During a distinguished career in Canadian journalism, Whyte served as executive editor of *Alberta Report* and *Western Report* magazines, editor in chief of *Saturday Night* magazine, founding editor of the *National Post*, and editor in chief and publisher of *Maclean's*. He was president of Rogers Publishing Limited, Canada's largest magazine company, and senior vice president of Public Policy at Rogers Communication.

In 2008, Whyte published *The Uncrowned King: The Sensational Rise of William Randolph Hearst*, which was a *Washington Post* Book of the Year. His second book, *Hoover: An Extraordinary Life in Extraordinary Times*, was a finalist for the National Book Critics Circle Award.

CHAPTER 35

FRANKLIN ROOSEVELT

The Great Depression

By Amity Shlaes

A great commander in chief abroad does not always make a great president at home.

That is the case when it comes to Franklin Delano Roosevelt.

In the 1940s, President Roosevelt led us to victory in World War II. That stunning achievement, however, obscures Roosevelt's record in the 1930s, when he battled the Great Depression at home—and met defeat.

To understand how this happened, it helps to remember who Roosevelt was before he became president.

His passion was the sea. An experienced sailor, he knew every crack and cranny of the Atlantic coast. His first work in the federal government was as assistant secretary of the navy, where his mastery of the seas became evident to colleagues.

After serving as governor of New York, Roosevelt was elected president in 1932. The job confronting him was all land. America lay mired in the Great Depression. One in four was unemployed. Roosevelt made a promise: to put Americans back to work. He would help "the forgotten man," the "man at the bottom of the economic pyramid."

To rescue America, the new president decided to steer the country like a ship in a storm, with himself as captain.

Just as a commander calms a nervous crew, Roosevelt told Americans to forget their fear. The only thing to fear, he said, was fear itself. Roosevelt also promised to rerig the economy and run it tight as a ship.

Roosevelt called his rerig the New Deal, and made its military aspect explicit: this was "a call to arms" he said. The Depression was an emergency for which Roosevelt claimed broad executive power. The downturn should be treated like a "foreign foe."

Perhaps because Roosevelt didn't like economics very much, the captain recklessly steered the economy into uncharted waters. Roosevelt opted for a command-and-control philosophy, never before tried in peacetime, and he gave himself the broadest possible license—a license to pursue, as he put it, "bold, persistent experimentation."

Roosevelt called for the government to manage industry.

New laws ordered companies to raise prices and wages—even when they couldn't afford to do so. He slammed individual businessmen. He called big corporations "enemies of peace."

Roosevelt was a man born into wealth. He imagined that he and his senior crew, his brain trust, could run the economy better than entrepreneurs.

For example, the new National Recovery Administration decided everything, down to how many logs a lumberyard could cut, and at what time—or how many chickens a butcher might sell.

But in the storm of the 1930s, few dared mutiny. Maybe this was the way economies were now supposed to work. That's what Roosevelt's "experts" said.

Roosevelt subsidized farmers and created temporary jobs in the arts; social work experienced a boom. He promised pensions to seniors. That sounded good. And the New Deal backed organized labor's demands for much higher wages. The recovery was just around the next bend, Roosevelt promised. All Americans had to do was wait for it.

As the years passed, however, the recovery stayed away.

For an economy is not like a battleship. An economy is more like a human. It makes choices. You can't command an economy to grow—the economy has to feel like growing. Under the New Deal, the economy instead felt like hiding belowdecks. What company would hire up if it couldn't pay the wages? Today we consider 6 percent unemployment a crisis. The overall unemployment stayed above 10 percent throughout the decade.

So if the New Deal broke its own promise, why did America give Roosevelt a second term in 1936?

One answer was that Roosevelt was indeed a charismatic captain, a man who did inspire. The new medium of radio allowed him to connect to millions of Americans merely by speaking into a microphone.

Second, Roosevelt convinced the nation that crisis was indeed the new normal.

Third, money was involved—the New Deal systematically rewarded voting blocs, whether seniors, laborers, or farmers. These groups expressed their thanks with their votes.

And finally, Roosevelt was a man of extraordinary personal will. Confined to a wheelchair by polio, Roosevelt did not allow obstacles, political or otherwise, to deter him. If he wanted something, he went after it and usually got it. That included his New Deal.

By the 1940 election, the big issue was a war across the Atlantic. Here was a realm where a navy man was a strong choice. And once Roosevelt turned to war, he eased up on business and instead hired companies to build him ships, planes, and guns.

Still, the facts are important to remember. We can praise President Roosevelt's war service all we like. But there's no way around that New Deal record. President Franklin Roosevelt himself put the "great" in the Great Depression.

Amity Shlaes is the acclaimed author of several *New York Times* bestsellers, including *The Forgotten Man: A New History of the Great Depression*, *Coolidge*, and *The Greedy Hand: How Taxes Drive Americans Crazy*. She is also the author of *Great Society: A New History*, a comprehensive account of the Johnson administration's most notable legacy.

Shlaes chairs the board of the Calvin Coolidge Presidential Foundation, a national foundation based at the birthplace of President Coolidge. The foundation's goal is to share Coolidge with Americans, by hosting debate and events at the Coolidge site and through newer media.

She has been a syndicated columnist for more than a decade. Her pieces have appeared in *National Review*, *Forbes*, Bloomberg News, the *Wall Street Journal*, *Foreign Affairs*, and the *American Spectator*.

Shlaes is a graduate of Yale College.

CHAPTER 36

FRANKLIN ROOSEVELT

Preparing for War

By Arthur Herman

In May 1940 the Nazi blitzkrieg was overrunning France. Great Britain would be next.

British Prime Minister Winston Churchill sent a telegram to the American president, Franklin Roosevelt.

"I trust you realize," Churchill wrote, "the voice and the force of the United States may count for nothing if they are withheld too long."

Roosevelt was a former assistant secretary of the navy and a student of naval strategy. If Hitler were to take control of Britain, he would take control of the Atlantic. This, Roosevelt knew, would pose a grave threat to America.

Roosevelt also knew America wasn't ready for war—not psychologically (most Americans didn't want to get involved in a conflict on the other side of the ocean) and not militarily.

The United States had the world's eighteenth-largest army. Hungary and even Holland had bigger armies, while Hitler commanded the most advanced military machine ever seen.

The army's chief of staff, General George Marshall, told Roosevelt that if Hitler overran Europe and landed seven divisions on the East Coast, there was nothing anyone could do to stop him.

With all this staring Roosevelt in the face, it would have been irresponsible for the commander in chief not to arm the United States for war.

But how?

Many in his administration believed then, as many Americans believe now, that the only way to deal with an extreme crisis was to give the government as much power and authority as possible.

But FDR had the insight to realize that a massive wartime buildup during what was still peacetime wouldn't succeed unless he harnessed the productive power of American business; that is to say, American free market capitalism.

The federal government could help coordinate industry's efforts; it could make sure resources like steel and aluminum got to the places where they were most needed, but otherwise the government would have to back off.

To the president who had created an alphabet soup of federal agencies to dig the country out of the Great Depression, this was about as un-Roosevelt as you could get.

But to his everlasting credit, the president realized that what he and the Democrats had tried with the Depression and failed—to manage the economy through government decree—wasn't going to work when it came to preparing for war.

The man Roosevelt called for help was General Motors CEO William Knudsen, a Danish-born immigrant who had worked his way up from the Brooklyn shipyards to head the largest automobile company in the world.

Knudsen told the president that if he gave him eighteen months, America would have more planes, tanks, and warships than it would know what to do with.

Roosevelt gave Knudsen what he wanted. In one of his most famous radio speeches in December 1940, a year before Pearl Harbor, the president told the American people that "we must be the great arsenal of democracy." He backed up his words with action.

In January 1941, defense spending rose to triple what it had been the previous six months. By July it quintupled; by December it jumped another twelvefold.

The factories, plants, and shipyards of America, the isolationist nation still at peace, was fast approaching Nazi Germany in its defense output. In 1942, it would blow past it. Before that year was out the United States was producing more war materiel than all three Axis powers—Germany, Italy, and Japan—combined.

All this was achieved through the miracle of mass production, which could exponentially produce more of something while simultaneously making it cheaper and faster. To cite just one dramatic example, the Saginaw Steering Gear Company contracted to make 280 Browning machine guns by March 1942. When that date came, it shipped twenty-eight thousand guns instead.

By then, of course, the United States, following the attack on Pearl Harbor, was fully engaged in the war—both in the Pacific and in Europe.

In every town in every state, manufacturers large and small turned their focus to making the weapons their sons and husbands and brothers would need to win the greatest armed conflict in history.

By 1944, American mills were producing 150 tons of steel every minute. Factories were building a plane every five minutes; and shipyards were launching fifty merchant ships a day, eight aircraft carriers a month.

Two-thirds of all war materiel used by the Allies in World War II came from America's plants and workers—one of three of those workers, it should be noted, were women.

And this was all made possible because a president learned from his past mistakes and had the courage to meet a new situation with a new idea. His closest advisors wanted him to put all his chips on government control, but he chose to bet the future of freedom on American capitalism instead.

He won.

And so did the world.

⁛

Arthur Herman is a Senior Fellow and director of the Quantum Alliance Initiative at the Hudson Institute. His research programs analyze defense, energy, and technology issues.

Herman is the author of nine books, including the *New York Times* bestseller *How the Scots Invented the Modern World*, the Pulitzer Prize finalist *Gandhi and Churchill: The Epic Rivalry That Destroyed an Empire and Forged Our Age*, and *Freedom's Forge: How American Business Produced Victory in World War II* (which *The Economist* named one of its Best Books of 2012).

Herman is a frequent contributor to *Commentary*, *Mosaic*, the *National Review*, the *New York Post*, and the *Wall Street Journal*. He was also the first non-British citizen to be named to the Scottish Arts Council from 2007 to 2009. He received his B.A. from the University of Minnesota and Ph.D. from Johns Hopkins University in history and classics.

CHAPTER 37

HARRY TRUMAN

Dropping the Bomb

By Elizabeth Spalding

Who was Harry Truman?

The American people didn't really know.

He had been vice president for all of eighty-two days.

And now, on April 12, 1945, upon Franklin Roosevelt's death, Truman had become the thirty-third president of the United States, the commander in chief of the biggest army in the world, in the biggest war in history, and was about to make some of the biggest decisions any president would ever make.

"Is there anything I can do for you?" Truman asked the late president's wife, Eleanor, upon his arrival at the White House to take the oath of office.

"Is there anything we can do for you, Harry? For you are the one in trouble now."

Harry Truman was born on May 8, 1884, in a small farm village in southwestern Missouri. His values—faith, hard work, and common sense—came from the middle of the middle of America. It's the key to understanding this straightforward, but complex man.

He never finished college, not because he wasn't capable—he was a voracious reader of history, biography, and the classics—but because his family needed his income, and family loyalty always came first.

He expected to be a farmer, just like his father and his father's father.

But that path changed in April 1917, when the United States entered World War I. Truman, then thirty-three, enlisted.

Truman commanded an artillery battery. His unerring tactical instinct and coolness under fire earned him the respect of his men. That loyalty never faded. The friendships he made during the war lasted a lifetime.

Truman returned home transformed: more confident, more worldly, and more ambitious. Now that he had seen Paris, he wasn't going back to the farm.

In 1919, he married his hometown sweetheart, Elizabeth "Bess"

Wallace. That same year, he opened a men's clothing store with an army friend, Eddie Jacobson.

After a successful first year, the enterprise failed when the country fell into a postwar recession. Truman refused to declare bankruptcy, though he was almost $20,000 in debt. It took him thirteen years to pay it back.

During this period, Truman came to the attention of Tom Pendergast, the powerful Democratic Party boss of Kansas City. Pendergast recognized a natural politician when he saw one.

Truman rose from county judge in 1923 to US senator in 1935. So close was his association with his political patron that his opponents mocked him as "the senator from Pendergast."

Once again, it was a world war that transformed him. He turned the chairmanship of an obscure committee into a national platform. It was officially known as the Senate Special Committee to Investigate the National Defense Program, but everyone called it the Truman Committee.

Its purpose was to investigate waste and incompetence in the war effort—and there turned out to be a lot. By forcing defense contractors to meet minimum quality standards, Truman not only saved taxpayers billions but saved thousands of lives.

In 1944, President Roosevelt, despite his failing health, sought a fourth term. He wanted to see the war to its end. To win what promised to be a close election, the party bosses felt FDR needed a new running mate. They worried that the current vice president, Henry Wallace, with his very Progressive views, would turn off moderate voters.

The moderate, Midwestern Truman, buoyed by the positive press from his committee work, seemed to be an ideal fit.

Wallace was out. Truman was in.

That fall, the Roosevelt-Truman ticket won handily.

FDR barely acknowledged Truman's existence, sharing nothing about war strategy—and nothing about the development of a new secret weapon, the atomic bomb.

And then Roosevelt died.

Truman had to get up to speed on everything—fast.

In less than four months, he made monumental decisions, not only on the direction of the war, but on the direction of the world.

He confirmed the US commitment to a new international organization, the United Nations.

He authorized the use of the atomic bomb against Japan.

On this agonizing decision, he never hesitated. Advised that Japan had no intention of surrendering, and, consequently, that an invasion of Japan would cost millions of American and Japanese lives, the choice for Truman was obvious.

"It was a terrible decision," he later wrote. "But I made it . . . and I'd make it again. . . ."

When the war finally ended with Japan's surrender on August 15, 1945, Truman had to figure out how to bring home 16 million servicemen and integrate them back into a peacetime economy.

The feisty Midwesterner met these challenges and more. The famous sign on his desk, "The Buck Stops Here," was no mere ornament. He lived it.

But there were many more "bucks" to come. A new war was looming, and Truman would soon be tested again.

A lifelong educator and frequent public speaker, Elizabeth Spalding is a Visiting Fellow at Hillsdale College's Van Andel Graduate School of Government. She is a Senior Fellow at the Pepperdine University School of Public Policy, and she serves as the chairman of the Victims of Communism Memorial Foundation, where she is also founding director of the Victims of Communism Museum.

Spalding is the author of *The First Cold Warrior: Harry Truman, Containment, and the Remaking of Liberal Internationalism* and the coauthor of *A Brief History of the Cold War.* Her scholarly and popular articles have been published widely, including in *Journal of Church and State*, the *Wilson Quarterly*, the *American Spectator*, *Law & Liberty*, and *Claremont Review of Books*.

Spalding holds a Ph.D. and an M.A. in international politics and political theory from the University of Virginia and a B.A. in politics from Hillsdale College.

CHAPTER 38

HARRY TRUMAN

Containing Communism

By Elizabeth Spalding

Upon learning of Franklin Roosevelt's death on April 12, 1945, Harry Truman was reported to have said, "I felt like the moon, the stars, and all the planets had fallen on me."

It was only a slight exaggeration.

The decisions the thirty-third president had to make in just the next four months would have crushed any normal person.

Managing the German surrender in May 1945, authorizing the use of the atomic bomb to end the war in the Pacific in August, and converting the economy from wartime to peacetime are just a sample of what he had to contend with.

It was also becoming clear that the Soviet Union was not going to be a partner in the postwar world. It was going to be an adversary bent on world domination.

Truman wasn't about to let this happen.

The first order of business was to save Western Europe. Eastern Europe was already gone.

As Winston Churchill vividly described in March 1946, ". . . an iron curtain has descended across the Continent."

Truman agreed with Churchill, committing the United States to containing the Soviet threat. This became known as the Truman Doctrine.

Around the same time, Truman's most trusted advisor, Secretary of State George Marshall, returned from Europe deeply concerned. He found Germany in ruins, England bankrupt, and France and Italy in chaos. Marshall reported it would take an unprecedented effort by the United States to breathe life into a moribund European economy. Failure to do so would hand over the Continent to the Soviets.

Truman authorized $13 billion in economic aid, a phenomenal

figure for the time. This became known as the Marshall Plan. And indeed, it accomplished its goal: the recovery of Europe, thwarting Soviet expansionism.

In May 1948, a new crisis emerged: a war was raging between the Arabs and the Jews. The UN was looking for a solution. The question before Truman: Should the United States recognize the new state of Israel?

Marshall argued no. It would further antagonize Arab states. But Truman saw a moral issue—the Jews had suffered enough over the centuries, most especially in the recent Holocaust—as well as a biblical and historical issue: this was the Jews' ancient homeland.

Thanks to Truman, on May 14, 1948, America became the first country to recognize the Jewish state.

One month later, Soviet leader Joseph Stalin took aim at the Marshall Plan. He cut off access to the free, western half of Berlin, located deep in Soviet-dominated East Germany.

The Communist dictator was gambling that the American president wouldn't defend the city, but Truman called his bluff. "We stay in Berlin. Period."

Truman ordered an airlift that, over fifteen months, completed more than 250,000 flights and delivered over 2 million tons of food, fuel, and supplies to beleaguered Berliners.

Stalin backed down.

One might therefore assume that Truman would have had an easy time winning the presidency in the upcoming 1948 election.

But so much economic turmoil at home—one labor strike after another, and one crisis after another abroad—made it difficult for Americans to appreciate Truman's accomplishments.

He didn't help himself by insisting that the armed forces and the federal judiciary be racially integrated. These were controversial decisions, but Truman thought they were right.

Facing a popular Republican opponent, New York Governor Thomas Dewey, and with his own party split by pro-segregationists and Progressives, Truman was in a very deep hole.

Undaunted, he embarked on a whistlestop campaign across the country, giving fiery speeches and traveling some twenty-two thousand miles—almost the equivalent of circling the globe.

It all seemed to no avail. When *Newsweek* polled fifty pundits three weeks before the election, everyone predicted a Truman defeat—which made his upset victory all the sweeter, a moment immortalized by his gloating over a *Chicago Tribune* headline that prematurely declared, "Dewey Defeats Truman."

Truman hardly had time to catch his breath before the next crisis.

The following year, 1949, the Soviets acquired the atomic bomb, and the Communists took over China, the most populous country in the world. Fortunately, that April, Truman had overseen the creation of the North Atlantic Treaty Organization, to defend against the Soviet threat.

Then, in June 1950, the North Korean Communists invaded South Korea, seeking to impose their totalitarian system over the entire peninsula.

It was another agonizing decision: to yield Korea and, consequently, much of Asia to the Communists or fight.

Truman chose to fight. The price was very high. Almost thirty-seven thousand Americans died in a conflict that lasted three years. South Korea was saved. And America's commitment to defending freedom could no longer be questioned. But it cost Truman his popularity.

When he left office, his approval rating was 22 percent, the lowest in American history.

It would take decades before Truman's reputation recovered. Churchill, who knew him well, never had any doubts about the man from Missouri's place in history, declaring in early 1953 that Truman "more than any other man . . . saved Western civilization."

A lifelong educator and frequent public speaker, Elizabeth Spalding is a Visiting Fellow at Hillsdale College's Van Andel Graduate School of Government. She is a Senior Fellow at the Pepperdine University School of Public Policy, and she serves as the chairman of the Victims of Communism Memorial Foundation, where she is also founding director of the Victims of Communism Museum.

Spalding is the author of *The First Cold Warrior: Harry Truman, Containment, and the Remaking of Liberal Internationalism* and the coauthor of *A Brief History of the Cold War*. Her scholarly and popular articles have been published widely, including in *Journal of Church and State*, the *Wilson Quarterly*, the *American Spectator*, *Law & Liberty*, and *Claremont Review of Books*.

Spalding holds a Ph.D. and an M.A. in international politics and political theory from the University of Virginia and a B.A. in politics from Hillsdale College.

CHAPTER 39

DWIGHT EISENHOWER

War Hero to President

By John Yoo

The Allies defeated the Axis powers—Germany and Japan—in World War II in no small part because of America's brilliant generals—men like George Marshall, George Patton, Douglas MacArthur, Omar Bradley, and Dwight Eisenhower.

Of that illustrious group, only one—Eisenhower—reached America's highest office, serving as the thirty-fourth president of the United States.

What made him stand out among his contemporaries?

Dwight David Eisenhower was born on October 14, 1890. Young Dwight, or "Ike," as he came to be known to everyone, was the third of seven children—all boys.

Of his childhood, the future president would later say, "We were very poor, but the glory of America is that we didn't know it. . . ."

Looking for a ticket out of his hometown of Abilene, Kansas, Ike entered the US Military Academy at West Point in 1911. He did little to distinguish himself academically, focusing more on football than his studies.

Upon graduating as a second lieutenant, he was posted to Fort Sam Houston in San Antonio, Texas. There, he met the petite, vivacious, and charming Mamie Doud. The daughter of a prosperous businessman, Mamie was used to cooks and servants but gave it all up for the spartan life of a military spouse when she married Ike in 1916. She would spend the next two decades moving from one dreary army base to the next. But as long as she was with her husband, she was happy. "Ike was my career," she said years later.

When America entered World War I in 1917, Eisenhower, to his frustration, was ordered to remain stateside to train others for combat. It was a bitter blow, and it set the pattern of Eisenhower's life for twenty years. As others rose to senior positions, his career stalled. He seemed destined to serve great men, not to be one.

From 1935 to 1939, Eisenhower worked as Douglas MacArthur's top aide in the Philippines, where they helped train the local army, giving the young man from Abilene his first real taste of international politics.

MacArthur was an extremely difficult personality who almost drove Ike to his wit's end.

But in retrospect, dealing with hard cases like MacArthur proved to be a blessing in disguise. If he could handle the egotistical general, he could handle anyone, including Winston Churchill, Franklin Roosevelt, and even Joseph Stalin. But that was in the future.

When the Japanese bombed Pearl Harbor on December 7, 1941, Eisenhower was a brigadier general. As impressive as that might sound, he was hardly at the top of anyone's list. His leadership skills, however, had not escaped the notice of the ever-shrewd George Marshall, Roosevelt's top military advisor.

In June 1942, much to the surprise of almost everyone, Marshall appointed Eisenhower commander of all US troops in Europe, elevating him over 366 more senior officers. It proved to be one of the best, if not the best, personnel decisions of the war.

Over the next thirteen months, Eisenhower oversaw the invasions of North Africa, Sicily, and Italy. There were many setbacks, many unforeseen disasters, many miscalculations, but Eisenhower never lost his composure, never lost his confidence that his men would prevail. And in each case, they did.

The main event, the invasion of France, however, was still ahead, and it needed a commander. President Roosevelt had no shortage of accomplished generals to choose from—MacArthur, Patton, Bradley—but he went with Ike.

Operation Overlord, or D-Day, as it is famously known, would be the largest amphibious invasion in history, with 150,000 men from over a dozen countries, 50,000 vehicles, 11,000 planes, and 6,000 naval vessels attacking the Nazis head-on.

But how to get them all across the English Channel before Hitler and his Nazi forces could counterattack?

It was a logistical and strategic nightmare, a high-stakes roll of the dice. And the outcome fell on one man's shoulders.

No one knew that better than Eisenhower. He prepared a letter assuming full responsibility in the event of failure. Tucking it in his wallet, he gave the go-ahead on June 6, 1944.

That letter never saw the light of day. The invasion succeeded. The letter is now archived in Eisenhower's presidential library.

The war ended eleven months later on May 8, 1945.

Eisenhower returned to the US a hero.

Both parties saw him as a future political star. However, no one knew whether he was a Republican or a Democrat. Sitting President Harry Truman so respected Eisenhower that he offered to serve as Eisenhower's vice president if the general wanted to run on the Democratic ticket in 1948. But Ike turned everybody down. Instead, he accepted an offer from Columbia University to be its new president.

By 1952, however, he was of a different mind.

The worsening Cold War with the Soviet Union convinced him that he had to get back into the fray.

Waiting until the last possible moment, he declared himself a Republican and entered the presidential race. The Grand Old Party was elated. It quickly made him its standard-bearer.

Eisenhower's campaign slogan, "I Like Ike," fit the mood of the nation perfectly.

His opponent in the general election, the Democrat, Adlai Stevenson, the erudite governor of Illinois, had little chance.

Eisenhower won easily.

America had elected a warrior to bring them peace.

John Yoo is the Emanuel Heller Professor of Law at the University of California at Berkeley. He is also a Nonresident Senior Fellow at the American Enterprise Institute, and a Visiting Fellow at the Hoover Institution, Stanford University.

He is the author of *Defender in Chief: Donald Trump's Fight for Presidential Power*; *Striking Power*; *Point of Attack: Preventive War, International Law, and Global Welfare*; and *Crisis and Command: A History of Executive Power from George Washington to George Bush*.

Yoo has published more than one hundred articles in academic journals on subjects including national security, constitutional law, international law, and the Supreme Court. He also regularly contributes to the *Wall Street Journal*, the *New York Times*, the *Washington Post*, the *Los Angeles Times*, and *National Review*, among others.

He graduated from Harvard University with a B.A. in American history, then earned a J.D. from Yale Law School.

CHAPTER 40

DWIGHT EISENHOWER

A General Keeps the Peace

By John Yoo

When Dwight Eisenhower, or "Ike," as he was universally known, was elected the thirty-fourth president of the United States in 1952, the American people weren't exactly sure who they had voted for.

He ran as a Republican, but was he a conservative? A moderate? A liberal?

Ultimately, it didn't really matter. The decorated World War II general who had waged war now promised to wage peace. And the voters trusted he would keep that promise.

Their trust was not misplaced. His first major act as president was to resolve the conflict in Korea that had begun in 1950 and cost America thirty-six thousand lives.

Here's how he did it: he made it clear to the Chinese, North Korea's patron, that if they didn't agree to a cease-fire, he would not hesitate to use nuclear weapons.

Soon after, an agreement was reached, drawing a line between North and South Korea at the 38th parallel. That agreement stands to this day.

Would Eisenhower have actually followed through on his threat? We'll never know, but that was the whole point.

"After Ike made peace in Korea," Eisenhower biographer Jean Smith wrote, "not a single American died in combat for the next eight years."

Throughout his time in office, he was urged to use American military power to resolve conflicts. And for eight years he resisted.

In 1953, the French wanted him to come in on their side in Vietnam.

In 1955, Chiang Kai-shek, the ruler of Taiwan, wanted America's help to take on Communist China.

In 1956, the Hungarians wanted him to back their revolt against Soviet rule.

Each supplicant made a good case for American intervention. Each time, Eisenhower refused to commit American troops. If he didn't see a clear path to victory, the risk, in his mind, was greater than the reward.

And even though he said he was prepared to use nuclear weapons, he greatly feared their destructive power.

To that end, he sought a treaty with the Soviets to end the arms race. He proposed that the US would open up all its military facilities to Russian inspection—provided the Soviets did the same. But the Soviet leader Nikita Khrushchev declined. He dismissed the proposal as an American trick to spy on the Soviet Union. It wasn't a trick. Eisenhower really meant it.

If Khrushchev wouldn't make a deal, Eisenhower would do what he had to do: make sure that America's nuclear capacity far outstripped the Soviets.

But while he recognized the Soviet threat, he didn't blindly accept the advice of his military chiefs. As a career soldier, he knew that the armed services always assumed the worst about an adversary's capabilities—the better to boost their budgets. But Eisenhower never took the bait. In fact, he trimmed portions of the military budget repeatedly during his tenure. He famously worried about what he coined the "military-industrial complex."

He brought the same pragmatism to the domestic front. His philosophy here was not much different than his foreign policy philosophy: if he could keep the country out of war—in this case, political war—everything else would take care of itself.

This worked brilliantly in his handling of the bombastic Republican senator from Wisconsin, Joseph McCarthy. McCarthy became nationally renowned for his thinly evidenced exposés of Communist infiltration in the American government.

There was Communist infiltration in the government, but McCarthy, unfortunately, might have been the worst person to lead that fight.

For example, he accused General George Marshall—the architect of the Allied victory in World War II, trusted advisor to Presidents Roosevelt and Truman, and one of the greatest secretaries of state in

American history—of being pro-Communist, an accusation that enraged Eisenhower.

Ike's advisors implored him to go on the offensive and attack the Wisconsin senator head-on, but that wasn't Eisenhower's style. He knew it was just a matter of time before McCarthy would hang himself.

He was right. McCarthy couldn't prove his accusations, was censured by the full Senate, and eventually drank himself to death in 1957.

This was vintage Ike: accomplishing goals without a lot of fanfare.

But if he needed to make a public show of force, he would. He sent federal troops to enforce a court ruling to integrate schools in Little Rock, Arkansas. Eisenhower has been criticized, and perhaps rightly so, for moving too slowly on civil rights issues, but he feared social upheaval if he did so. And the truth is, blacks made significant economic progress in the postwar decades. Between 1940 and 1960, the black poverty rate fell from 87 percent to 47 percent.

Government projects actually got done. Eisenhower conceived of and began the Interstate Highway System, which changed America probably more than any other single infrastructure project in American history, and on which we all still depend.

He did it despite a Democratic majority in the House and Senate during his last six years as president. For Eisenhower, it was about getting the job done, not who got the credit.

Indeed, the Eisenhower years are widely regarded as the period in which America was truly great—a time when it dominated the world in almost every respect, from science to culture, from John Wayne westerns to commercial aviation.

The warrior had kept his promise. He kept the peace.

John Yoo is the Emanuel Heller Professor of Law at the University of California at Berkeley. He is also a Nonresident Senior Fellow at the American Enterprise Institute, and a Visiting Fellow at the Hoover Institution, Stanford University.

He is the author of *Defender in Chief: Donald Trump's Fight for Presidential Power*; *Striking Power*; *Point of Attack: Preventive War, International Law, and Global Welfare*; and *Crisis and Command: A History of Executive Power from George Washington to George Bush*.

Yoo has published more than one hundred articles in academic journals on subjects including national security, constitutional law, international law, and the Supreme Court. He also regularly contributes to the *Wall Street Journal*, the *New York Times*, the *Washington Post*, the *Los Angeles Times*, and *National Review*, among others.

He graduated from Harvard University with a B.A. in American history, then earned a J.D. from Yale Law School.

CHAPTER 41

JOHN F. KENNEDY

A Star Is Born

By Larry Elder

On the morning of November 22, 1963, the United States was at the peak of its power. It dominated the world in every respect—militarily, economically, and culturally. Nothing seemed out of America's reach, even the moon.

The man guiding the ship of state was movie-star handsome, youthful (only forty-six), and always seemed to know what to say and how to say it.

That man was John F. Kennedy, the thirty-fifth president of the United States.

JFK was born just outside of Boston on May 29, 1917, the second of nine children. His father, Joe Kennedy, made a fortune trading stocks, selling whiskey, and financing movies. A noted philanderer, his affair with actress Gloria Swanson was the stuff of Hollywood legend.

He parlayed his financial success into political success, eventually serving as Franklin Roosevelt's ambassador to Great Britain.

Joe expected much from his sons, but most especially from his eldest son, Joe Jr.

When young Joe died in Europe during World War II, the burden of the father's ambitions fell on his second son.

But there was no certainty that John, known to his family and friends as "Jack," would survive the war.

Some months earlier, when his PT boat was rammed by a Japanese destroyer in the South Pacific, it was assumed that he and his entire crew had been killed. But through Kennedy's heroic efforts, all but two were rescued.

For his bravery, Jack was awarded the Navy and Marine Corps Medal.

Living up to his father's expectations and using the connections of his maternal grandfather, John "Honey Fitz" Fitzgerald—a former mayor of Boston—Kennedy was elected as a Democrat to Congress in 1946.

Kennedy was just twenty-nine.

But he already had his eyes on a bigger prize. In 1952 he was elected to the US Senate.

One year later, he married the beautiful socialite Jacqueline Bouvier. Their wedding was the major event of the 1953 social season. There were seven hundred guests at the ceremony and twelve hundred at the reception.

With his new wife and new Senate seat, Kennedy was making all the right moves. Bored by the endless committee meetings in Congress, he focused on increasing his national profile, traveling around the country, giving speeches, and appearing on talk shows to discuss current events.

With his distinct Boston accent, he developed a dynamic speaking style that, coupled with his good looks and beautiful young family, made him picture-perfect for the new age of television.

He positioned himself as a centrist on domestic policy and a staunch anti-Communist on foreign policy.

By 1960, he was ready to make his presidential move. While his critics argued that, at age forty-three, he was too young and inexperienced for the nation's highest office, Kennedy argued that it was time for a new generation to take charge.

With his shrewd and loyal brother Bobby running his campaign, Kennedy won the Democratic nomination. But the race against Richard Nixon, Dwight Eisenhower's vice president, would prove to be much tougher.

Two things stood in his way. One was his Catholic faith: more than a few Americans wondered whether Kennedy would be more loyal to the pope than to the Constitution. The other was the charge that he was much less experienced than his opponent.

He dealt with the first problem by confronting it head-on.

"No one asked me my religion in the South Pacific" was his mic-drop response. It worked.

He dealt with the second objection by debating Nixon four times—the first televised presidential debates ever. Positioning himself to the right of Nixon on the Communist threat, his command of the facts was impressive.

Even more impressive was how he looked on camera: cool, collected, and charismatic. Nixon, in contrast, looked tired and pale.

Still, with all that, Kennedy barely managed to squeak out the win.

It was so close that many urged Nixon to contest the results, but Nixon refused. He didn't want the country distracted in the middle of the Cold War.

Kennedy got off to a great start with one of the most stirring inaugural addresses in American history. The most famous line was, "Ask not what your country can do for you—ask what you can do for your country."

Lines like this inspired millions, not only in the US but around the world, and helped to create the Kennedy mystique.

There were muscular lines, too, such as America would "pay any price, bear any burden, meet any hardship, support any friend, oppose any foe to assure the survival and success of liberty."

But lofty rhetoric, Kennedy soon learned, was no substitute for rigorous planning.

His first attempt to promote liberty was a disaster—the April 1961 Bay of Pigs invasion to oust Cuban Communist leader Fidel Castro. Concocted by the CIA, it was supposed to look like a homegrown Cuban uprising, but nothing went as planned and Kennedy soon became disenchanted.

When the CIA-trained invaders, Cuban exiles, failed to secure a beachhead, Kennedy refused to order air support.

Many of the exiles were slaughtered. The rest were captured by Castro's military.

It was a humiliating defeat and bolstered the critics who said that he was too young and inexperienced to be president.

Were they right?

The nation wouldn't have to wait long to find out.

Larry Elder is a nationally syndicated talk show host, bestselling author, and filmmaker. His published books include *The Ten Things You Can't Say in America*, *Showdown*, and *What's Race Got to Do with It? Why It's Time to Stop the Stupidest Argument in America*, and *Dear Father, Dear Son*.

His acclaimed documentary *Uncle Tom* (2020) has been shown in film festivals around the world.

Elder attended Brown University, receiving a B.A. in political science. He then attended the University of Michigan School of Law.

CHAPTER 42

JOHN F. KENNEDY

Young President in Crisis

By Larry Elder

Everything about John F. Kennedy, the thirty-fifth president of the United States, was appealing: his good looks; his glamorous wife, Jackie; their picture-book children, Caroline and John Jr.

JFK personified how America wanted to see itself: youthful, forward-looking, confident.

But Kennedy had his doubters.

Did he have the maturity and experience to lead the most powerful nation on earth?

Early on, it seemed the answer was no. Within three months of taking office, he botched his first major foreign policy test, a poorly planned attempt to overthrow the Communist government in Cuba. The failure, now known as the Bay of Pigs fiasco, was an international embarrassment.

His meeting in Vienna in June 1961 with Soviet leader Nikita Khrushchev didn't help matters. Khrushchev pushed Kennedy around like a playground bully.

These early failures might have broken a lesser man, but Kennedy, a World War II navy combat veteran, turned out to be made of very stern stuff. The next confrontation with the Communists would be different.

That confrontation happened in October 1962. Khrushchev, thinking he could intimidate Kennedy again, ordered the secret installation of nuclear-armed missiles in Cuba, just ninety miles from the Florida coast.

Kennedy ordered a blockade of the island, insisting that the missiles be immediately removed. What ensued was a high-stakes standoff—the Cuban Missile Crisis. Kennedy's advisors estimated 80 million Americans would die if war broke out. The Soviets could expect even worse losses.

The world held its breath.

This time, it was the Soviet dictator who blinked. The missiles were removed.

The world breathed a huge sigh of relief, and America could get on with its seemingly limitless future because there would actually be a future.

Kennedy called his vision the New Frontier. It would feature significant tax cuts to get the economy roaring again, an ambitious national project—land a man on the moon by the end of the decade—and more progress on civil rights.

When Kennedy entered office, marginal tax rates were ridiculously high—up to 91 percent for personal income; 52 percent for corporate. This was somewhat alleviated by various deductions, but as Kennedy noted, the high rates stunted "the growth of profits and pay checks."

Another way to unify the nation was to create a national project everyone could get behind, something that would appeal to America's can-do spirit. It would also be a way to demonstrate that American capitalism could do things that no other economic system could. Russia had taken an early lead in the space race. Kennedy was determined that America should leave the Russians in the space dust.

"We choose to go to the moon in this decade and do the other things, not because they are easy, but because they are hard . . . because that challenge is one that we are willing to accept, one we are unwilling to postpone, and one which we intend to win. . . ."

But there was another challenge back on earth that would be equally hard, and that would be to guarantee civil rights for all Americans.

Kennedy had to walk a political tightrope. He needed the Southern vote and the Southern vote was still largely for segregation. He also believed the best way to remedy discrimination was to improve the economic lot of all American citizens.

"There is little value," he said, "in a Negro's obtaining the right to be admitted to hotels and restaurants if he has no cash in his pocket and no job."

Although Kennedy didn't move as fast on civil rights issues as many of his advisors wanted, he clearly recognized that something had to be done.

In 1963, he gave a televised speech to the nation in which he said, "Are we to say to the world, and much more importantly, to each other that this is the land of the free except for the Negroes . . . ? [T]he time has come for this nation to fulfill its promise."

With Kennedy at the helm, it all seemed possible—ever higher levels of prosperity, the moon landing, and progress toward racial equality.

It really did seem like a modern version, as Jackie put it, of Camelot, a popular Broadway play at the time. Instead of King Arthur, there was JFK. Instead of Guinevere, there was Jackie. Instead of the Knights of the Round Table, a cadre of Ivy League–trained advisors.

By the fall of 1963, with the next election less than a year away, a second term seemed to be a lock.

And then on November 22, it all came to a tragic end.

As his motorcade drove through downtown Dallas, Kennedy was shot and killed by an angry, avowed Communist by the name of Lee Harvey Oswald.

JFK's assassination didn't merely shock the nation—it shattered it. The Camelot dream broke into a million pieces.

It's no exaggeration to say that Kennedy's sudden death was the single most traumatic event in America in the twentieth century, not because it was the worst event, but because there was nothing anyone could do to make it right.

The nation would never be the same.

Larry Elder is a nationally syndicated talk show host, bestselling author, and filmmaker. His published books include *The Ten Things You Can't Say in America*, *Showdown*, and *What's Race Got to Do with It? Why It's Time to Stop the Stupidest Argument in America*, and *Dear Father, Dear Son*.

His acclaimed documentary *Uncle Tom* (2020) has been shown in film festivals around the world.

Elder attended Brown University, receiving a B.A. in political science. He then attended the University of Michigan School of Law.

CHAPTER 43

LYNDON B. JOHNSON

The Not-So-Great Society

By Amity Shlaes

We are living in Lyndon Johnson's America."

That's what a staffer of the thirty-sixth president once said. It's still true today.

Consider America's out-of-control federal debt. We'd like to reduce it.

But we can't. Because doing so means taking down institutions that seem as permanent as the Rockies.

Medicare.

Medicaid.

And many other entitlements.

All these institutions were established by Lyndon Johnson.

The slogan of John F. Kennedy, Johnson's predecessor, was a "New Frontier." By this, Kennedy meant more opportunity to enable Americans to thrive, not massive federal programs that would bankrupt our grandchildren.

Kennedy advocated significant tax cuts.

Even Kennedy's signature project emphasized symbolism: get a man on the moon—to show the Soviet Union, and American citizens, what America can do for itself.

But an assassin's bullet felled Kennedy in 1963.

And now it was Johnson's turn.

Johnson didn't have to set a new agenda: he could have simply completed what Kennedy had already set in motion.

And that's what he did . . . at first. For example, he saw those Kennedy tax cuts into law.

But Johnson didn't want to be a caretaker. He wanted to be a historymaker.

So Johnson created a program called the "Great Society." Not only would he outdo John Kennedy. He would outdo his own hero, Franklin Roosevelt.

At the University of Michigan in 1964, Johnson announced dramatic plans to change life "in our cities, in our countryside, and in our classrooms."

Later, Johnson promised to "cure" poverty. Note the verb: not "alleviate," not "relieve," but "cure."

Johnson, with his long career as a congressman and a senator, was genuinely great at one thing: passing laws.

And pass them he did.

A civil rights law to banish inequality.

A voting rights law to end the voting gap between white and black Americans.

A law to provide health care for seniors—Medicare.

A law to provide health care for disadvantaged families—Medicaid.

And laws that built out modern entitlements such as food stamps and public housing.

It all sounded great.

The American people agreed.

After serving the remaining months of Kennedy's term, Johnson easily won election in his own right in 1964. Then Johnson felt even freer to set his own course. Between 1965 and 1968 Johnson brought hundreds of social programs to life.

But who would manage these programs? And how would government employees do it? No one knew.

No matter. They could work out the details later.

Johnson was always in a rush. His aide, Joseph Califano, said there was never enough for Johnson. The man adopted new programs the way a child eats chocolate-chip cookies.

What mattered most to Johnson were the noble intentions of these programs. But those intentions didn't lead to Great Society heaven.

Riots in American cities did not stop after Johnson passed his civil rights and entitlement laws. Riots increased. Life in public housing projects got worse. The Great Society institutionalized incentives for young woman to have children out of wedlock.

Still, these benefits came to look like mountain rocks: hard to cut. Johnson's successor, Richard Nixon, a Republican, increased spending on Great Society projects faster than Johnson.

Down the decades we have spent billions and then trillions. Yet today we can see that the results of the Great Society were anything but great.

Crime and high taxes plagued the cities.

Poverty refused to be cured.

Entitlements didn't free families: entitlements shackled families to poverty.

Student scores on standardized tests dropped after 1965. Even today the most Progressive politicians would agree that public school systems in major cities are failing.

Medicare certainly feels kind to senior citizens. But it places a burden of debt on our grandchildren that is anything but kind.

People think of Franklin Roosevelt as the father of our nation's social programs. But today we spend more on Great Society programs than on those of the New Deal.

These facts may surprise many Americans. We hear all the time that the Great Society was a great success. Perhaps that's because romanticizing government intervention is a rule in public radio and television—both institutions made possible through a 1967 law signed by Johnson.

Today might be the moment to clear our heads.

And the moment to take the Great Society record seriously.

After all, these edifices are not the Rockies. Medicaid, Medicare, and our social programs can be changed. Our debt can be reduced.

Yes, we are living in Lyndon Johnson's America. But that doesn't mean we have to.

Amity Shlaes is the acclaimed author of several *New York Times* bestsellers, including *The Forgotten Man: A New History of the Great Depression*, *Coolidge*, and *The Greedy Hand: How Taxes Drive Americans Crazy*. She is also the author of *Great Society: A New History*, a comprehensive account of the Johnson administration's most notable legacy.

Shlaes chairs the board of the Calvin Coolidge Presidential Foundation, a national foundation based at the birthplace of President Coolidge. The foundation's goal is to share Coolidge with Americans, by hosting debate and events at the Coolidge site and through newer media.

She has been a syndicated columnist for more than a decade. Her pieces have appeared in *National Review*, *Forbes*, Bloomberg News, the *Wall Street Journal*, *Foreign Affairs*, and the *American Spectator*.

Shlaes is a graduate of Yale College.

CHAPTER 44

LYNDON B. JOHNSON AND THE VIETNAM WAR

By Bill Whittle

It was 2:38 p.m. Central Standard Time on November 22, 1963. President John F. Kennedy was dead, assassinated less than two hours earlier.

In the cramped quarters of a blue and white Boeing 707, with the call sign Air Force One, Vice President Lyndon Baines Johnson took the oath of office. He was now the thirty-sixth president of the United States.

He was born just 207 miles to the southwest, in a dusty patch of road called Stonewall, Texas, on August 27, 1908. Lyndon Johnson's childhood was spent in what biographer Robert Caro described as "a land without electricity, where the soil was so rocky that it was hard to earn a living from it."

Unlike the perfectly groomed, somewhat aloof Kennedy, Johnson was a classic backslapping, handshaking politician. Everything Johnson did had Texas dust on it.

In his run for the US Senate in 1948, following eleven years in the House of Representatives, Johnson drew huge crowds by showing up at campaign events in a never-before-seen, by-God actual helicopter, which he named the "Johnson City Windmill."

Out of 1 million votes cast, Johnson won the Democratic Senate primary by a mere 87 votes. Beating his Republican opponent in the general election proved to be much easier. Only forty years old, the Texan of humble origins was now a member of the most exclusive club in America.

By the late 1950s, Lyndon Baines Johnson—universally referred to as LBJ—had become arguably the most effective Senate majority leader in the country's history. This was due in large part to the bullying, flattering, and intimidating one-on-one sessions that became known as "The Treatment." He would back his target into a corner; poke him in the chest; threaten, cajole, even weep. He'd wax exuberant one moment, be scornful the next, complain, promise, compliment, and curse.

And he almost always got what he wanted.

During his six years as president, he was preoccupied with two things: his Great Society project—hundreds of social programs he was convinced would end poverty—and the Vietnam War.

LBJ didn't end poverty, and he didn't end the Vietnam War. But the Vietnam War ended LBJ.

The origins of the war can be traced to the Communist takeover of China in 1949 and the Chinese-backed North Korean invasion of South Korea the following year. If South Vietnam were to fall to the Communist North, it was logical to assume that Laos, Cambodia, Thailand, Malaysia, Indonesia, and the rest of Southeast Asia would topple in turn—a potential catastrophe known as the Domino theory.

Johnson firmly believed in the Domino theory, as most foreign policy experts did, but couldn't bring himself to make a firm commitment to win the war. His heart was in his Great Society programs. He didn't want to get bogged down in a conflict on the other side of the world.

But ironically, he ensured that's exactly what would happen by pursuing an incremental, half-in, half-out strategy.

Johnson personally selected the next day's airstrike targets from the isolation of the White House Situation Room often in his pajamas. "Those boys can't hit an outhouse without my permission," he once said. He wasn't exaggerating—it was literally true.

This might have been the worst possible way to fight against a light, fast, and imaginative enemy.

Here are just three examples of the kind of restrictions that Lyndon Johnson imposed upon American forces fighting in Vietnam:

Retreating enemy soldiers could be fired upon only with the intent to wound by aiming at the lower extremities.

Aircrews could not shoot at surface-to-air missile sites unless the SAMs shot first.

And both Hanoi—the enemy capital—and Haiphong—their major port—were off limits completely.

This war needed to be fought. America was defending South Vietnam against a brutal Communist invasion from North Vietnam just as it had defended South Korea against a brutal Communist invasion from North Korea. The tragedy was that such a morally justifiable war was fought so incompetently, ineptly, and absurdly.

The problem was Johnson. He didn't see the conflict as a war; he saw it as a negotiation. Unfortunately for Johnson, the United States, and the South Vietnamese people, the North Vietnamese were immune to "The Treatment." Every cease-fire, every bombing halt was perceived as weakness, another opportunity to resupply and rearm. Johnson's political inclination was to give the North Vietnamese what they wanted and thereby negotiate a deal. But the North Vietnamese didn't want a deal. They wanted Vietnam. All of it.

Johnson was trapped. He couldn't win the war, and he couldn't get out of it.

As more and more American soldiers came home in body bags—the total would come to over fifty-eight thousand—as antiwar campus protests raged across the country, and as the press turned against him, Johnson's popularity plummeted.

By the next election in 1968, both LBJ and the American people had had enough.

On March 31, 1968, Johnson shocked the nation and his own closest advisors when he announced on television "I shall not seek, and I will not accept, the nomination of my party for another term as your president."

He had outdone his hero, Franklin Roosevelt, with his Great Society programs, but he was undone by a foreign war in a faraway country.

Bill Whittle is a writer, film director, and historian. Since 2010, Whittle has been writing and producing critically acclaimed video content.

His *Firewall* segments have been seen by millions, as have his multiple series on the *Daily Wire*, including *Apollo 11: What We Saw*, *The Cold War: What We Saw*, and *An Empire of Terror: What We Saw.*

CHAPTER 45

UNDERSTANDING NIXON

By Hugh Hewitt

Name this president.

He created the Environmental Protection Agency and put real teeth into the Clean Air Act. Environmentalists called him the most environmentally conscious national figure since Teddy Roosevelt.

He was admired, sometimes revered, by civil rights leaders, including Martin Luther King and Jackie Robinson. He desegregated Southern schools and vigorously enforced civil rights laws, often against his own political interests.

His grasp of foreign affairs was acknowledged by both friend and foe to be unmatched. He opened US relations with Communist China, signed the first nuclear disarmament agreement in history, and ended the Vietnam War. When the peace accords were signed, it was clear that America was the victor in the conflict.

Did you guess our thirty-seventh president, Richard Nixon?

If not, don't feel bad. Most people know only one thing about him—that he resigned from office following the Watergate scandal.

Looking back, his offense—covering up for overzealous subordinates who were caught trying to steal campaign secrets from the Democrats—almost seems quaint. But at the time, it roiled the nation.

Had he accepted responsibility, apologized early on, he almost certainly would have survived. Sadly, he never considered the idea. When he felt cornered, his first reaction was to counterattack, not apologize.

Nixon was first and always a fighter. Everything he ever achieved he had to fight for.

He was born on January 9, 1913, in Yorba Linda, California, in a small house his father built from a mail-order kit. Yorba Linda is now a bustling suburb of Los Angeles, but then it was basically a lemon grove with a road running through it. He grew up with no advantages. If he wanted to escape, he read.

He read a lot.

It's part of the Nixon legend that he attended a local college, Whittier. What isn't well known is that he was accepted to Harvard. He didn't attend only because his parents couldn't afford to send him there.

After volunteering for service in the navy in the South Pacific during World War II, he returned home. A small-town law career, not politics, looked to be his future.

Then fate took a hand. The local Republican Party was searching for a fresh face to oppose a popular Democratic congressman. Nixon passed the audition. Nobody expected him to win, but nobody expected him to campaign as hard and as effectively as he did.

He quickly became a fast-rising political star, achieving national attention when he almost single-handedly exposed a major State Department official, Alger Hiss, as a Soviet spy. Hiss was everything Nixon was not—sleek, urbane, Ivy League–educated. He was well known and well loved among the East Coast intellectual and media elite. No one in Hiss's social set believed the charges against him—until Nixon forced them to.

The liberal elites never forgave him for that or for beating the glamorous and very Progressive Hollywood actress Helen Gahagan Douglas, in the 1950 California Senate race.

In 1952, Dwight Eisenhower tapped him to be his running mate.

In just six years, Nixon rose from a small-town lawyer to vice president of the United States. He was only thirty-nine.

Ike sent his vice president on important diplomatic missions all over the globe. It was on these missions that Nixon developed his mastery of international affairs.

After a heartbreaking loss to John F. Kennedy in the presidential election of 1960, one of the closest and most disputed elections of the modern era, Nixon returned to California. There he lost another election, an ill-advised run for governor in 1962.

He should have been done as a politician.

He wasn't.

In one of the most unlikely comebacks in American political history, Nixon won the Republican nomination for president in 1968 and then defeated incumbent vice president Hubert Humphrey in the general election.

Few presidents have ever walked into a more difficult situation. The country was in turmoil. Bobby Kennedy and Martin Luther King had both been assassinated within the year, just weeks apart. The Vietnam War was raging, student unrest was out of control, and the economy was floundering.

Nixon expertly navigated the turbulent political waters, steering a centrist course—just what his devoted supporters, the people he called the "Silent Majority" wanted him to do.

What he believed in—a sense of duty, common decency, hard work, the inherent greatness of America—they believed in. The press never liked Nixon, but the majority of the American people loved him. He was reelected in 1972 in one of the biggest landslides in American history, winning forty-nine of the fifty states.

He ended the military draft, brought the Vietnam War to a close in early 1973, and later that year saved Israel by airlifting military supplies during the so-called Yom Kippur War.

And then came Watergate.

Now you know why Richard Nixon—truly Shakespearean in both his attributes and his flaws—may be America's most misunderstood—and underappreciated—president.

Hugh Hewitt is a nationally syndicated talk show host and bestselling author. His books include *The War Against the West* and *The Queen: The Epic Ambition of Hillary and the Coming of a Second "Clinton Era."*

Hewitt is also a professor of law at Chapman University and a widely published columnist. He is a former president of the Richard Nixon Foundation. He spent six years in the Reagan administration, including a stint in the White House counsel's office.

Hewitt is a graduate of Harvard and the University of Michigan Law School.

CHAPTER 46

GERALD FORD

Healing a Divided Country

By Hugh Hewitt

The date was August 9, 1974.

Something had just happened that had never happened before.

An American president, Richard Nixon, resigned, forced out of office by a political scandal forever known as "Watergate."

The nation was in a bad way: the fate of the Vietnam War remained uncertain, the economy was in a recession, and faith in the basic government institutions was almost nonexistent.

America was coming unglued.

Gerald Ford, now the thirty-eighth president of the United States, would have to hold it together.

And that's exactly what he did.

In his first speech after being sworn in, Ford declared that "our long national nightmare is over."

It was what the American people needed to hear.

Ford was no stranger to adversity. He was born in Nebraska on July 14, 1913—the child of an abusive alcoholic father.

His mother, to save her son and herself, fled to Grand Rapids, Michigan. After divorcing Gerald's father, she married again. This time she got it right. Her new husband, the owner of a paint store, raised young Gerald as his own.

Gerald grew into a popular, handsome, and athletic young man.

A star football player in high school and college, he won back-to-back national championships with the University of Michigan team in 1932 and 1933.

Recruited by the Detroit Lions and Green Bay Packers, Ford reluctantly turned them down. He was set on a career in law.

He worked his way through Yale Law school, supplementing his earnings by modeling. A photo of Ford and his girlfriend even made the cover of *Cosmopolitan*.

After passing the bar, Ford set up shop in his hometown of Grand Rapids.

But like millions of others at the time, his plans were interrupted by the Second World War. Shortly after Pearl Harbor, Ford joined the navy and saw considerable action in the South Pacific.

He returned home convinced that America could not retreat into isolationism as it had after World War I. If peace and freedom were to be preserved, America would have to preserve them. The voters of Grand Rapids agreed. In 1948, they elected him to Congress as a Republican.

His easygoing personality quickly earned him friends on both sides of the political aisle, including fellow navy veterans John Kennedy and Richard Nixon.

Ford summed himself up as "a moderate in domestic affairs, an internationalist in foreign affairs, and a conservative in fiscal policy."

By 1965, he had worked his way up to Republican minority leader, but his ultimate goal was to become Speaker of the House.

To achieve that goal, however, the Republicans would have to win a majority of seats.

But in election after election, they failed.

Even in 1972, when Ford's longtime friend President Richard Nixon won reelection in a landslide, the Republicans still could not take that majority in the House.

After that, Ford gave up. He told his wife, Betty, that he planned on serving only one more term.

Fate had other plans.

In October 1973, Vice President Spiro Agnew resigned—the result of a bribery scandal. The Twenty-Fifth Amendment required Nixon to nominate a new vice president, subject to congressional approval.

Weakened by Watergate, Nixon asked House and Senate leaders of both parties who they would approve.

Gerald Ford was the almost unanimous choice.

Nixon, of course, hardly considered the possibility that he would have to resign. And Ford hardly considered the possibility that he would become president.

But that's exactly what happened.

Ford became the first and only chief executive to ascend to the office without winning a single vote for vice president or president.

Initially, Americans were pleased with their new captain. Ford came across as honest, genial, and well adjusted. He personified the American middle class: a devoted husband and father of four.

But Watergate refused to go away. The media that hounded Nixon out of office wanted blood: they wanted Nixon tried, convicted, and behind bars.

Ford saw it differently. One month into his term, he decided to spare the nation from further turmoil and division. Against the advice of nearly all his advisors, Ford pardoned Nixon for Nixon's involvement in the Watergate scandal.

If the pardon spared the nation, it did not spare Gerald Ford. His popularity plummeted almost overnight.

And that was not his only crisis.

He had to get America out of Vietnam. But how? The overwhelmingly Democratic Congress demanded a sudden and complete withdrawal. Ford said no and warned of disaster.

The Democrats refused to listen. They got the victory they wanted—defeat in Vietnam. With Ford's hands tied, the South was left to fend for itself. North Vietnam and its Vietcong allies overran the South in a matter of months.

There was one other catastrophe in Ford's administration. It came from an unexpected source—a new late-night comedy show called *Saturday Night Live*. Taking one stumble on an airport tarmac as their inspiration, the comedy troupe turned the former star athlete into a clumsy buffoon.

Despite reducing inflation, standing firm against an aggressive Soviet Union, and steadily rebuilding the nation's morale, Ford could not overcome the Nixon pardon and his *SNL* image. He lost a close election to Georgia Governor Jimmy Carter in 1976.

In his inauguration speech, Carter had the grace to acknowledge Ford's legacy, thanking him "for all he has done to heal our land."

History has confirmed Carter's judgment.

Hugh Hewitt is a nationally syndicated talk show host and bestselling author. His books include *The War Against the West* and *The Queen: The Epic Ambition of Hillary and the Coming of a Second "Clinton Era."*

Hewitt is also a professor of law at Chapman University and a widely published columnist. He is a former president of the Richard Nixon Foundation. He spent six years in the Reagan administration, including a stint in the White House counsel's office.

Hewitt is a graduate of Harvard and the University of Michigan Law School.

CHAPTER 47

JIMMY CARTER

Farmhouse to White House

By Tevi Troy

In 1974, the *Atlanta Journal Constitution* headlined a story, "Jimmy Who Is Running for What!?" The "who" was Jimmy Carter, the governor of Georgia, and the "what" was the presidency of the United States.

Carter could always count on people to underestimate him. This was one of the keys to his success.

He would outsmart, outwork, and outhustle his opponents. By the time they realized he was gaining political ground, he had already sped past them.

Jimmy Carter was born on October 1, 1924, to a prosperous farming family in Plains, Georgia. His father, Jimmy Sr., was an unabashed racial segregationist, but his mother was of a different temper. She was well known in the town for inviting blacks into the Carter home. During her son's presidency, she became famous in her own right as the ever-quotable "Miss Lillian." When asked why someone wouldn't vote for her son, she quipped, "Some people are just dumb."

In 1943, Carter was admitted to the Naval Academy. Graduating near the top of his class, he decided to go into the submarine service. In 1952, he transferred into the recently formed nuclear sub program, mastering the technical aspects of nuclear engineering.

Then in the middle of an already brilliant naval career, Carter stunned everyone when he gave it all up. After his father's unexpected death in 1953, Carter abruptly returned to Georgia with his wife, Rosalynn, to manage the family peanut farm.

During these years, Carter was under a lot of pressure to join the town's White Citizens' Council. It certainly would have been good for business, but it would have violated his principles, and that's something Carter would never do. He was a Southerner—no doubt about that—but he was always his own man.

As was his wont, as soon as Carter succeeded in one thing, he wanted to do something else. That something else was politics. He ran for the Georgia state legislature in 1962 and ran for Georgia governor in 1970.

Then, in 1976, he ran for president of the United States. He won all of those contests.

In the aftermath of the Watergate scandal that toppled President Richard Nixon, Carter had the perfect message: "I'll never lie to you." That message led him to victory against incumbent President Gerald Ford, making Carter the thirty-ninth president of the United States, and the first true outsider to occupy the White House since Abraham Lincoln.

As president, Carter brought his boundless energy to bear, not only on the nation's problems but the world's. He wanted to solve everything all at once: peace in the Middle East, an end to antagonism with the Soviet Union, a foreign policy making human rights America's first priority, and a new era of racial harmony at home.

But it was too much. Almost everything he tried blew up in his face. The man who had always been underestimated overestimated his ability to control events. There were two notable exceptions—one foreign and one domestic.

The foreign exception was the peace treaty he mediated between Israel and Egypt in 1978. Carter worked tirelessly to bring the two sides to a workable compromise. Given that the two nations had fought a war only five years before, it was a major achievement. The cold peace that resulted endures to the present day.

The domestic exception was the deregulation of the airline industry. Since the 1930s, the federal government set fares, routes, and schedules. Carter's new policy liberated the airlines to figure this out for themselves. The result was an increase in competition and drastically lower airfares. A mode of transportation for businessmen became a mode of transportation for everyone.

These were rare triumphs in an otherwise troubled administration. Every week seemed to bring more bad news: stagflation (a recession and inflation happening at the same time), crippling energy shortages leading to long lines at gas stations, and a Soviet invasion of Afghanistan were just a few examples. These weren't all Carter's fault, but his tone-deaf reading of the national mood was a self-inflicted wound.

This was best illustrated in his controversial 1979 "Malaise speech," in which Carter called for gasoline rationing and chided the American people for being materialistic. Not surprisingly, it didn't wear well. The country wanted inspiration and got a sermon instead.

The nail in Carter's political coffin came later that year: the Iran Hostage Crisis. It began with Carter's decision to admit the exiled Shah of Iran to the United States for cancer treatment. The shah, a long-standing American ally, had fled his throne ahead of Iran's Islamic Revolution. Angered by Carter's hospitality toward their former monarch, radical Muslim students took over the US embassy and captured sixty-six Americans, fifty-two of whom were held hostage for a seemingly interminable 444 days. In April 1980, Carter authorized a military rescue operation, but it was poorly planned and poorly executed, ending in complete—and completely humiliating—failure. America had never seemed more impotent.

By November 1980, the nation was ready for a change. Ronald Reagan, with his natural ebullience and message of optimism, swept Carter out of office, winning forty-four out of fifty states, sending him into the longest-ever post-presidency. It was a bitter pill for the successful naval engineer, peanut farmer, and Georgia politician to swallow.

At least he could say this, though: history would never again ask, "Jimmy Who?"

Tevi Troy is a presidential historian and bestselling author. His latest book is *Fight House: Rivalries in the White House from Truman to Trump.*

Troy has extensive White House experience, having served in positions including deputy assistant and then acting assistant to the president for domestic policy.

He is the author of *What Jefferson Read, Ike Watched, and Obama Tweeted*; *Intellectuals and the American Presidency*; and *Shall We Wake the President?* He has written over 250 articles for the *New York Times*, the *Wall Street Journal*, the *Washington Post*, and *National Review*. He has appeared on CNBC, CNN, C-SPAN, FOX News, FOX Business, and *NewsHour*, among other outlets.

Troy has a B.S. in industrial and labor relations from Cornell University and an M.A. and Ph.D. in American civilization from the University of Texas at Austin.

CHAPTER 48

RONALD REAGAN

The Great Communicator

By Scott Walker

Ronald Reagan fashioned his political career and his presidency around three things.

1. *Lower taxes*
2. *Smaller government*
3. *Strong defense*

In doing so, he almost single-handedly resurrected and redefined the modern conservative movement. But he did much more than that—he resurrected and redefined America.

If that sounds like an impressive feat, it was. And it's hard to imagine anyone other than Reagan who could have done it. Known by friend and foe alike as the "Great Communicator," even Democrats conceded that no one could connect with the American people like Reagan. Whenever he went on TV—which was often—to promote a policy, he invariably swung the American people his way. When he explained something, it just made sense.

Fittingly, it was a TV speech in 1964 entitled "A Time for Choosing" that launched his political career. He delivered it on behalf of Republican presidential candidate Barry Goldwater. Here's just one of his many memorable passages.

"No government ever voluntarily reduces itself in size. . . . Actually, a government bureau is the nearest thing to eternal life we'll ever see on this earth."

This was pure Reagan: a basic truth delivered with humor.

Born in a small Midwestern town on February 6, 1911, Reagan honed his communication skills as a radio announcer, and then as an actor. He was a genuine Hollywood star and celebrity for over two decades before he got into politics. Tall, broad-shouldered, and handsome with a golden voice, he was well respected and well liked by his peers. He was also seen as a natural leader. From 1947 to 1952, he was president of the Screen Actors Guild, deftly guiding it through the blacklist era.

In 1965, encouraged by the positive response to his "A Time for Choosing" speech, Reagan decided to run for governor of California. He won easily. The victory immediately established him as a major figure in the Republican Party. By 1980, he was their overwhelming choice for president.

That year, he soundly defeated President Jimmy Carter. The incumbent lost because his pessimistic approach to problem-solving mirrored the justifiably sour mood of the country. The economy was going nowhere, caught in the double grip of inflation and stagnation.

In contrast, Reagan—ever the optimist—offered a way out. It wasn't the American people who were to blame, he told voters, it was the government. Reagan would get it out of the way. He would lower taxes and cut red tape.

He did both.

The media dismissed his plan, calling it "Reaganomics." But it worked.

From 1982 to 1987, the American economy, defined as GDP adjusted for inflation, rose an astonishing 27 percent, manufacturing 33 percent, and the median income by 12 percent.

An estimated 20 million new jobs were created. All income classes and all racial and ethnic groups benefited from the Reagan economy.

The dark decade of the seventies, a time in which it looked like America was in a terminal eclipse, faded away. It was, as Reagan put it, during his 1984 reelection campaign, "Morning in America" again.

Every bit as transformational as his work on the economy was his approach to foreign policy, specifically the Soviet Union. It's easy to forget, but when Reagan came to office in 1981, Soviet-style communism appeared to be as strong, if not stronger, than American-style democracy.

Whereas Reagan's predecessor had taken a "we just need to get along" approach, Reagan saw it much differently. He didn't mince words. In March 1983, he called the Soviet Union an "evil empire." The media and the Democrats wailed that the phrase was reckless, but it was typical Reagan. Simple, clear, and true. What else do you call a totalitarian system that had deprived millions of people across the globe of their freedom?

When asked what his strategy was for fighting the Cold War, Reagan replied. "We win. They lose."

It wasn't just a glib line. He meant it. He expanded the US defense budget to unprecedented levels, in part to develop a ballistic missile shield his critics dubbed "Star Wars." The strategy was to pressure the Soviets to try and keep up—which he knew they couldn't. He was right. They didn't have the money or the technology. Soviet premier Mikhail Gorbachev did all he could to pressure Reagan to drop it, but he would not budge.

To drive home his point, Reagan went to the Berlin Wall, a symbol of Communist oppression, and delivered one of his most famous lines: "Mr. Gorbachev, tear down this wall!"

By the end of the decade, a year after Reagan left office, the Soviet Union collapsed, an outcome no one could have imagined—except possibly Reagan himself. There are many reasons why this happened, but no one played a bigger role than our fortieth president.

We won. They lost.

Before the Reagan era, Americans were depressed and uncertain. By the end of it, they were optimistic and confident. Reagan had stuck to his formula: lower taxes, less government, strong defense. It worked.

And it still does today.

Governor Scott Walker was raised with a heart for public service, patriotism, and hard work. In June 1993, Walker was elected to the state assembly, where he helped lead the way on welfare reform, public safety, and education.

In 2002, he was elected to the Milwaukee County executive office. In this position, Walker faithfully kept his promise to spend taxpayer money as if it were his own. In 2008, he won reelection with nearly 60 percent of the vote.

In 2010, Walker was elected the forty-fifth governor of Wisconsin. He immediately implemented reforms to promote economic growth, fiscal order, and government accountability. He was reelected in 2014.

He is currently president of Young America's Foundation.

CHAPTER 49

GEORGE H. W. BUSH

Read My Lips

By Tevi Troy

In 1991, George H. W. Bush, the forty-first president of the United States, had a record-breaking approval rating of 89 percent. Less than two years later, he lost his reelection.

To understand how it happened, we have to understand the man—both his strengths and his weaknesses.

George H. W. Bush was born on June 12, 1924 to a storied New England family. His ancestor, Dr. Samuel Prescott, rode with Paul Revere in 1775 to warn his fellow American patriots of the British invasion. Bush's grandfather made a small fortune in the burgeoning steel business of the 1910s. His father, Prescott Bush, enlarged that fortune as a banker and later became a US senator.

Young George could have had a cushy life, but he didn't want it. After Pearl Harbor, he enlisted as soon as he could, becoming the youngest pilot in the US Navy. He wasn't yet nineteen years old. He flew fifty-eight missions. That he survived was a testament to his skill, fortitude, and some luck.

Following the war, and graduation from Yale (in two and a half years) he surprised everyone by moving his new wife, Barbara, and their young son, George W. Bush, to the middle of nowhere—Odessa, Texas. Rather than live off the family fortune, he decided to make his own fortune in the oil business.

It took a while, but he did it. In 1966, Bush sold his interest in the company he cofounded, Zapata Oil, to dedicate himself to a life in politics.

After losing a run for the Senate, he won a congressional election in suburban Houston. Recognizing a new political star, Republican leadership gave him a choice seat on the powerful Ways and Means Committee.

In Congress, Bush established a reputation as a political moderate, but one not afraid to take tough stances. For example, he was a strong supporter of civil rights legislation.

From Congress, Bush served in the Nixon and Ford administrations as UN ambassador, envoy to China, and director of the CIA, and then vice president for Ronald Reagan.

After that there was only one job left: president.

Despite having a reputation as a genuinely nice guy—he often sent handwritten notes to friend and foe alike—Bush was not afraid to throw sharp political elbows. In the 1988 presidential campaign, he painted his Democratic opponent, Massachusetts Governor Michael Dukakis, as a soft-on-crime liberal. The paint stuck. Bush won forty states.

Almost immediately, he achieved success in foreign policy.

First was his triumph in the Persian Gulf.

Following an unprovoked invasion of Kuwait by Iraqi dictator Saddam Hussein, Bush organized a thirty-four-country coalition to liberate Kuwait in Operation Desert Storm in January 1991. The coalition achieved an overwhelming military victory in less than two months. The swift win with few casualties also helped to end the "Vietnam Syndrome"—the idea that America no longer had the confidence to project its military power when provoked. In addition, respect for the armed services was restored.

Second, was Bush's masterful handling of the end of the Cold War, the dissolution of the Soviet Union, and the reunification of East and West Germany—all without firing a single shot. We take this for granted now, as if it was something preordained, but it could have easily spiraled into chaos or worse. By keeping a cool head, Bush made it possible for the Soviet empire to peacefully fade away. He stayed in close contact with Soviet leader Mikhail Gorbachev, and then his successor Boris Yeltsin, to make sure that the Russian nuclear stockpile remained fully secured.

With these achievements, it's not hard to explain why Bush, in March 1991, was polling as the most popular president ever to that time.

So what went wrong?

As good as Bush was with foreign policy, that was how much he struggled on the domestic side. Among his worst mistakes was going back on his famous campaign promise, "Read my lips. No new taxes." Given that he had to deal with Democratic majorities in both the House and the Senate, maintaining such a pledge would have been challenging, but breaking it severely damaged Bush's credibility.

It also didn't help that the nation fell into a recession. Suddenly, Bush was the silver-spoon guy who couldn't relate to everyday Americans' kitchen table concerns.

There was one domestic decision, however, that showed Bush at his finest: his nomination of Clarence Thomas for the Supreme Court. When Thomas was unfairly accused of sexual harassment during his confirmation hearing, there was a lot of political pressure on Bush to withdraw the nomination. But he never considered it. Bush gave Thomas his unwavering support, and Thomas was confirmed.

The election of 1992 came down to the economy. And here, despite the fact that recovery was well underway, Bush was unable to find his footing. He knew how to talk to foreign leaders, but he sometimes stumbled when talking to his fellow citizens.

Bush handled his election loss to Arkansas Governor Bill Clinton with his signature grace and class. But he got a measure of vindication eight years later when his son George W. succeeded Clinton as the forty-third president of the United States, making H. W. and G. W. the first presidential father-son pair since John and John Quincy Adams 172 years earlier.

Tevi Troy is a bestselling presidential historian and bestselling author. His latest book is *Fight House: Rivalries in the White House from Truman to Trump*.

Troy has extensive White House experience, having served in positions including deputy assistant and then acting assistant to the president for domestic policy.

He is the author of *What Jefferson Read, Ike Watched, and Obama Tweeted*; *Intellectuals and the American Presidency*; and *Shall We Wake the President?* He has written over 250 articles for the *New York Times*, the *Wall Street Journal*, the *Washington Post*, and *National Review*. He has appeared on CNBC, CNN, C-SPAN, FOX News, FOX Business, and *NewsHour*, among other outlets.

Troy has a B.S. in industrial and labor relations from Cornell University and an M.A. and Ph.D. in American civilization from the University of Texas at Austin.

CHAPTER 50

BILL CLINTON

The Comeback Kid

By Bill Whittle

Bill Clinton may have been the luckiest president in US history.

The forty-second president of the United States entered the White House just as the Cold War ended and left it just before the War on Terror began.

It was a time of unparalleled peace and prosperity, when America stood alone as the world's superpower. The Soviet Union had crashed and burned, and China was only just beginning to make its presence felt.

Given this opportunity, what would Clinton do with it?

William Jefferson Clinton was born on August 19, 1946, in Hope, Arkansas. There was nothing privileged about his background. Whatever he made of his life, for good or for ill, he did on his own. His father, a traveling salesman who had been married five times before the age of twenty-seven, died months before Bill was born. His mother soon remarried, but her second husband, an abusive alcoholic, wasn't exactly an upgrade from the first.

Yet somehow, young Bill managed to navigate his way through the wreckage. Blessed with a sharp mind and a winning personality, he developed a passion for politics early on, and found out he was good at it. He exuded likability.

In high school, he joined Boys Nation, a program where students learn how government operates. In 1963, the program allowed sixteen-year-old Bill to travel to the White House to meet America's charismatic young president, John F. Kennedy. On the bus ride home, the awestruck teenager vowed to a friend, "Someday, I'm going to have that job."

In 1964, he enrolled at Georgetown University. He majored in international affairs with an eye toward being a career diplomat. Four years later, he won a prestigious Rhodes Scholarship, allowing him to study at the University of Oxford in England.

By now, Clinton's trademark charm was readily apparent. At Yale Law School, he applied that charm on one of his fellow students, Hillary Rodham, a serious and ambitious young woman from Chicago. Clinton pursued her for four years before she finally agreed to marry him in 1975.

Like his hero JFK, Clinton wasted no time seeking public office. In 1974, at just twenty-eight, he ran as a Democrat for one of Arkansas's four congressional seats. Although he lost, he made a big impression. In 1978, he tried again—this time for the governorship. It was an audacious move, but he pulled it off, becoming one of the youngest governors in American history.

Nicknamed the "Boy Governor," Clinton made rookie mistakes, like raising an unpopular car registration tax. He lost his bid for reelection in 1980. He was now the youngest former governor in American history.

But Clinton was undeterred. Learning from his mistakes, he traveled up and down the state, working his charm on disaffected voters. And in 1982, he returned to the governor's mansion.

He would be reelected three more times.

Clinton governed as a centrist. He promoted liberal policies, such as affirmative action, but also conservative ones, such as raising the state's education standards, encouraging people to get off welfare, and supporting the death penalty.

At the dawn of the 1990s, Clinton's pragmatism began to attract the attention of Democrats outside of the South. Could Clinton be the savior they were looking for—a moderate who could lift the party out of its left-wing rut? The Democrats hadn't won a presidential election since 1976. Clinton, never short of self-confidence, thought he was the man for the job.

In 1991, he declared his intention to challenge Republican President George H. W. Bush. That year, Bush's approval rating had reached a sky-high 89 percent, thanks to his masterful handling of the Gulf War. Beating Bush seemed like a near-impossible task.

But first, of course, he would have to win the Democratic nomination.

Just as primary season began in earnest, his campaign hit a brick wall: an accusation of infidelity made by an Arkansas state employee named Gennifer Flowers.

On the popular TV news show *60 Minutes*, Clinton denied the affair but vaguely admitted to "causing pain" in his marriage.

Despite the deflection, the TV appearance convinced voters to give him another chance, earning him the nickname the "Comeback Kid." The Arkansas governor walked away with the nomination.

In the 1992 general election, he zeroed in on an economy that had fallen into a recession. His campaign manager, James Carville, kept the always-loquacious candidate on message: "It's the economy, stupid." Clinton made the sale, declaring to voters, "I feel your pain."

Perhaps most importantly, Clinton benefited from the third-party candidacy of Texas billionaire Ross Perot. Running on a platform stressing the national debt and the outsourcing of jobs to Mexico, Perot's campaign attracted many voters who otherwise would have voted for the Republican incumbent.

Split three ways, Clinton only won 43 percent of the vote, but it was enough to win an Electoral College landslide, 370 to Bush's 168.

Clinton had achieved his dream—he had John F. Kennedy's job. But he had no idea how hard that job would be.

Bill Whittle is a writer, film director, and historian. Since 2010, Whittle has been writing and producing critically acclaimed video content.

His *Firewall* segments have been seen by millions, as have his multiple series on the *Daily Wire*, including *Apollo 11: What We Saw*, *The Cold War: What We Saw*, and *An Empire of Terror: What We Saw*.

CHAPTER 51

BILL CLINTON

The Fall from Grace

By Bill Whittle

When Bill Clinton took office on January 20, 1993, at age forty-six, he was the first of his generation—the baby boomers born after World War II—to reach the White House.

The United States had recently won its four-decade-long Cold War with the Soviet Union, making it the dominant nation in the world. Everything seemed possible.

"There is nothing wrong with America," Clinton told the inauguration crowd, "that cannot be cured by what is right with America."

But nothing went right in Clinton's first few months on the job.

Intending to prove himself as a no-nonsense commander in chief, in the summer of 1993 Clinton ordered US troops to capture a troublesome warlord, Mohamed Farrah Aidid, in Mogadishu, Somalia. Despite the American soldiers' heroic efforts, it was a high-profile disaster. Eighteen Americans had died in the infamous "Black Hawk Down" incident, and, as a result, Clinton got cold feet. He immediately ordered the remaining troops out of the country. The new president looked like a hopeless amateur.

That perception only intensified when his proposal to take over the American healthcare industry, a full one-seventh of the economy, blew up in his face. Aiming to cement his place in history next to Democratic presidential icons Woodrow Wilson, Franklin Roosevelt, and Lyndon Johnson—all of whom massively expanded the reach of government in Americans' lives—Clinton sought to create a European-style universal healthcare system. He compounded his mistakes by putting his wife, Hillary, in charge of the project. Ultimately, the sheer size of the proposal (it was over thirteen hundred pages long and would cost hundreds of billions of dollars), and Hillary's lack of transparency (she held all her policy meetings in secret) provoked fierce opposition, sinking the bill.

It also led to massive Democratic losses in the 1994 midterms. The Democrats lost eight Senate seats and a staggering fifty-two House seats, giving Republicans control of both chambers for the first time in forty-two years.

The center of gravity in Washington suddenly shifted to the Republican House Speaker Newt Gingrich, the mastermind of the GOP tidal wave. When Clinton tried to assert his authority, he only sounded more desperate, insisting, "I am relevant. . . . A president . . . has relevance."

No one was listening. It very much seemed like Bill Clinton would be a one-term president.

But then, in April 1995, domestic terrorists blew up the Alfred P. Murrah Federal Building in Oklahoma City, killing 168 people, including 19 children. The nation went into shock and Clinton went into action. Suddenly he was everywhere, comforting both the residents of Oklahoma City and the American people. He was also steadfast in his conviction to capture and punish the perpetrators.

It was perhaps Bill Clinton's Finest Hour. America had a president again. And the president had a renewed sense of confidence.

He also had a new strategy: he would co-opt his opponents' best ideas. Guided by his savvy pollster, Dick Morris, he worked with Republicans in 1996 to reform welfare programs, requiring beneficiaries to find work. He deregulated the telecommunications and financial industries, opening up the economy. He signed the Communications Decency Act, which allowed free speech to flourish in the world's newest medium, the internet. In short, he returned to his centrist, pragmatic roots. Before long, it was the Republicans grasping for relevance.

Clinton's policies facilitated one of the longest peacetime economic expansions in American history, generated federal surpluses, and reduced the national debt. They also helped him sail easily to reelection in 1996, becoming the first Democratic president since Franklin Roosevelt to win a second term.

But just when it seemed like he had finally mastered the office, it all came crashing down . . . and he would have no one to blame but himself.

In January 1998, an obscure internet site called the Drudge Report revealed that Clinton had had an Oval Office affair with a twenty-two-year-old intern, Monica Lewinsky.

First, Clinton denied the rumors, then made matters worse by trying to lie his way out of the scandal. When called to testify under oath, he insisted that he never had a sexual relationship with "that woman."

Nobody believed him.

In December 1998, the House of Representatives impeached William Jefferson Clinton on a charge of perjury. It was the first presidential impeachment in 130 years.

Although the Senate Democrats ensured Clinton's acquittal in February 1999, the Lewinsky affair preoccupied the nation for over a year. Worse, it distracted Clinton from focusing on a very real threat: the Islamic terrorist group Al Qaeda. In August 1998, the group attacked US embassies in Kenya and Tanzania, killing over two hundred people. And then, in October 2000, Al Qaeda detonated a bomb next to USS *Cole*, a destroyer refueling at a port in Yemen, killing seventeen American sailors. And he balked at his chance to take out the then-unknown leader of this newest threat to America: a young Saudi radical by the name of Osama bin Laden.

And therein lies the real disappointment of the Clinton years. Although much was accomplished, so much more could have been done. Sadly, all most people remember about President Clinton is that he had a tawdry affair with a White House intern.

Bill Whittle is a writer, film director, and historian. Since 2010, Whittle has been writing and producing critically acclaimed video content.

His *Firewall* segments have been seen by millions, as have his multiple series on the *Daily Wire*, including *Apollo 11: What We Saw*, *The Cold War: What We Saw*, and *An Empire of Terror: What We Saw*.

CHAPTER 52

GEORGE W. BUSH

From Texas to Ground Zero

By Elizabeth Spalding

No one alive on September 11, 2001, will ever forget the shock and horror of that day.

The unthinkable happened: radical Islamic terrorists hijacked American airplanes and crashed them into buildings in New York and Washington, DC, murdering three thousand innocent people.

The attack shattered Americans' sense of security.

Surely another assault was coming. But when? Tomorrow? Next week? Next month?

The question preoccupied the nation's commander in chief, the forty-third president of the United States, George W. Bush.

If he had anything to say about it, "the inevitable" would never happen.

George Walker Bush was born in New Haven, Connecticut, on July 6, 1946. Although he came from a prominent New England and proud Republican family, his character was formed by his upbringing in Midland, Texas, where his father and future US President George H. W. Bush built a successful oil business.

A blue blood with a cowboy spirit, young George went to Yale and later Harvard Business School.

But instead of hitting the books, he hit the booze.

Not surprisingly, his grades suffered.

After graduating, he went into the Texas oil industry.

But unlike his father, he didn't find oil.

He did, however, find love. In 1977, he married Laura Welch, also of Midland, Texas. Four years later, they had two children, twin daughters Barbara and Jenna. Bush loved his family. But when he turned forty, he realized he had a drinking problem and needed to make a big change. With the help of family friend, the renowned Reverend Billy Graham, Bush became, in his words, a believing Christian. He never took another drink.

He channeled his newfound energy into his father's 1988 run for the presidency. Bush's folksy, gregarious charm proved to be an asset on the campaign trail. If he didn't have the family knack for finding oil, he did have the family knack for politics.

In 1992, his father lost his reelection to Democratic candidate Bill Clinton. Bush took it hard. But ironically, the defeat opened the door to his own political career.

With the help of gifted strategist Karl Rove, Bush ran for governor of Texas in 1994, taking on the popular incumbent, Democrat Ann Richards. She refused to take him seriously. This proved to be a fatal mistake. Promising to cut taxes and reform the state's education system, Bush won by a surprising margin, 54 percent to 46 percent.

He won again in 1998 by an even larger margin, making him the front-runner for the 2000 Republican presidential nomination.

Bush campaigned as a "compassionate conservative," seeking to unite the party's moderate and conservative wings and, beyond that, to appeal to Independents in a divided country. Although he faced a strong challenge from Arizona Senator John McCain, Bush won the nomination, setting up a showdown with Clinton's Vice President Al Gore in the general election.

Gore should have had the advantage, since he was an incumbent during a time of economic prosperity and peace. But his awkward, stiff personality turned off voters, while Bush's easygoing manner resonated with the average American.

The election ended up being one of the most controversial in US history. Bush assumed he had lost when the major television networks declared Florida for Gore. Without the Sunshine State, Bush had no path to victory. Then, in the middle of the night, the networks reversed themselves: Bush had won Florida and thus the election. Gore even called Bush to concede, only to retract his concession hours later.

Thirty-six days of recounts and lawsuits ensued. Throughout it all, Bush held on to his slim lead. In mid-December, the Supreme Court finally settled the contest in Bush's favor.

With little foreign policy experience, Bush entered office with an agenda weighted toward domestic issues: cutting taxes, improving education, reforming Social Security, and adding a prescription drug benefit for senior citizens.

On September 11, 2001, everything changed. As Bush was visiting an elementary school in Sarasota, Florida, to promote his education policies, his chief of staff whispered these fateful words in his ear: "America is under attack."

The president's safety uncertain, Bush was flown to a secure location in Nebraska, gathering as much information as he could. But by evening, at his insistence, he was back at the White House.

He addressed the nation at 8:30 p.m.: "These acts shattered steel, but they cannot dent the steel of American resolve."

Within three days, he was at the site of the New York attack, already known as "Ground Zero." With a bullhorn in his hand, Bush addressed a crowd of rescue workers. When one of them shouted, "We can't hear you," Bush responded with the most famous words of his presidency: "I can hear you! The rest of the world hears you! And the people . . . who knocked these buildings down will hear all of us soon!"

The crowd shouted back, "USA! USA!"

George Bush was now focused on one goal: keeping the nation safe.

Every day after 9/11 would be 9/12.

A lifelong educator and frequent public speaker, Elizabeth Spalding is a Visiting Fellow at Hillsdale College's Van Andel Graduate School of Government. She is a Senior Fellow at the Pepperdine University School of Public Policy, and she serves as the chairman of the Victims of Communism Memorial Foundation, where she is also founding director of the Victims of Communism Museum.

Spalding is the author of *The First Cold Warrior: Harry Truman, Containment, and the Remaking of Liberal Internationalism* and the coauthor of *A Brief History of the Cold War*. Her scholarly and popular articles have been published widely, including in *Journal of Church and State*, the *Wilson Quarterly*, the *American Spectator*, *Law & Liberty*, and *Claremont Review of Books*.

Spalding holds a Ph.D. and an M.A. in international politics and political theory from the University of Virginia and a B.A. in politics from Hillsdale College.

CHAPTER 53

GEORGE W. BUSH

The War on Terror

By Elizabeth Spalding

After radical Islamic terrorists struck the World Trade Center and the Pentagon on September 11, 2001, George W. Bush, the new forty-third president of the United States, swung into action. His every thought was about keeping America safe.

Supported by a highly experienced team consisting of Vice President Dick Cheney, Secretary of State Colin Powell, Secretary of Defense Donald Rumsfeld, and National Security Advisor Condoleezza Rice, Bush—himself a former Texas Air National Guard fighter pilot—declared a War on Terror. The real-life villain was Osama bin Laden, the leader of the Islamic terrorist group Al Qaeda and the mastermind of the 9/11 attack.

Bush emphasized that he would "make no distinction between the terrorists who committed these acts and those who harbor them." This put Afghanistan's Taliban regime, which had given Al Qaeda safe haven, in the crosshairs.

In October 2001, Bush ordered military action in Afghanistan. Within two months, the Taliban was overthrown, replaced by a new government friendly to the United States. Osama bin Laden, however, evaded capture.

Bush could have ended it there. But he worried that a new attack, perhaps of even greater magnitude, was inevitable. The main source of his fear was Saddam Hussein, the dictator of Iraq, and longtime sponsor of terrorism. With a history of violating UN resolutions and fierce antagonism to the US, Hussein boasted about his nuclear weapons program. The CIA and Great Britain's MI6 insisted it wasn't a bluff.

The United States, Bush argued, couldn't "wait for threats to fully materialize." He declared that if Iraq did not abandon its "weapons of mass destruction," America would act. When Hussein ignored him, Bush, with the support of both Republicans and Democrats, made good on his warning. In March 2003, US-led forces invaded Iraq. Within one month, Hussein was gone, and within two months, Bush stood on the deck of an aircraft carrier in front of a banner that declared, "Mission Accomplished."

Bush looked like a bold, decisive leader prepared to do whatever was necessary to protect the homeland. Voters rewarded him with a victory over the Democratic candidate, Massachusetts Senator John Kerry, in the 2004 presidential election.

As Bush's second term began, however, the situation in Iraq deteriorated. The original plan to depose Hussein had morphed into a plan to remake the country into the first Arab democracy. The idea, the thinking went, was that if Iraq could become democratic, other Arab countries would follow. America hastily organized a Western-style election, but Iraqis' tribal hatred for one another soon erupted. The US was caught in the crossfire. American casualties mounted monthly, and the American public soured both on the war and on the president they had recently reelected.

Bush's problems were compounded when, after an extensive search, no weapons of mass destruction were found, undermining the rationale for the invasion.

Things went from bad to worse in August 2005. A massive hurricane, Katrina, devastated New Orleans, killing over a thousand people and destroying billions of dollars in property.

The media blamed Bush. A photo of the president looking down on the city from Air Force One, rather than being on the ground with those suffering, became the disaster's defining image. That Bush couldn't control the weather and was not responsible for the city's inadequate infrastructure was ignored.

When things seemed like they couldn't get any worse, they did. In late 2007, the country was hit with a major financial crisis. Once again, Bush took the blame for something for which he was not responsible. For a decade, government policies—begun in the Clinton administration—encouraged banks to throw out the traditional lending standards by which they measured a homebuyer's creditworthiness. By the early 2000s, one could buy a home without making any down payment at all—something unheard of in previous generations. By the late 2000s, the bubble was ready to burst. When Bush refused to bail out Lehman Brothers, a legendary Wall Street banking firm enmeshed in home loans, it did.

Against his free-market instincts, Bush committed $700 billion to rescue the mortgage industry—an act some say saved the economy but left Main Street angry that it was footing the bill for an irresponsible Wall Street.

Bush's approval rating fell to a dismal 25 percent.

Yet amid all these setbacks, Bush did something quite extraordinary, an act of true courage. When almost all his advisors, both military and political, told him to cut his losses and accept defeat in Iraq, he refused. He believed that such an action would irreparably damage both America's security and credibility with its allies. Rather than drawing down forces, he decided in January 2007 to increase them—a strategy that came to be known as "the surge."

It worked. By the following year, American casualties had dramatically diminished.

When he handed the presidency over to his successor Barack Obama, there was a clear path forward for both Iraq and the US economy.

It was an impossibly difficult two terms, but Bush could point to one undeniable fact—after 9/11, there had not been another such attack on American soil.

A lifelong educator and frequent public speaker, Elizabeth Spalding is a Visiting Fellow at Hillsdale College's Van Andel Graduate School of Government. She is a Senior Fellow at the Pepperdine University School of Public Policy, and she serves as the chairman of the Victims of Communism Memorial Foundation, where she is also founding director of the Victims of Communism Museum.

Spalding is the author of *The First Cold Warrior: Harry Truman, Containment, and the Remaking of Liberal Internationalism* and the coauthor of *A Brief History of the*

Cold War. Her scholarly and popular articles have been published widely, including in *Journal of Church and State*, the *Wilson Quarterly*, the *American Spectator*, *Law & Liberty*, and *Claremont Review of Books*.

Spalding holds a Ph.D. and an M.A. in international politics and political theory from the University of Virginia and a B.A. in politics from Hillsdale College.

CHAPTER 54

BARACK OBAMA

"Hope and Change"

By Carol Swain

No American president entered the White House with more goodwill than Barack Obama. Even those who had opposed the new forty-fourth president during the 2008 election received him with pride.

The nation had elected its first black president—a historic event.

As Obama said in his victory speech, "If there is anyone out there who still doubts that America is a place where all things are possible, who still wonders if the dream of our founders is alive in our time . . . tonight is your answer."

Ironically, throughout his two terms as president, Obama disavowed the sentiment he had so eloquently expressed. We would later learn that the man whose triumph testified to America's greatness rejected America's greatness.

Barack Hussein Obama was born on August 4, 1961, in Honolulu, Hawaii. To say his background was eclectic would be an understatement. His mother, Ann Dunham, was married to Barack Obama Sr., an exchange student from Kenya. They divorced three years later.

In 1965, she would marry another exchange student, Lolo Soetoro. Mother and son went with him to Indonesia. Known as Barry Soetoro at the time, he attended both Catholic and Muslim schools in Jakarta.

His mother, unimpressed by the education he was getting in Indonesia, sent him back to Hawaii to live with her parents.

In 1979, he moved to the mainland, where he enrolled in Occidental College in Los Angeles.

It was jolting. Who was he? He didn't feel comfortable identifying as white or black. As he later wrote, "I hadn't grown up in Compton or Watts."

Restless, he transferred to Columbia University in New York City. While at Columbia, he apparently resolved his racial conflict. He would identify as African American even though he barely knew his father and had been raised primarily by his white grandparents. He was now Barack; Barry was gone.

In 1985, he took a job as a "community organizer" on the South Side of Chicago, but this, too, tried his patience. The incremental improvements to tenant rights or job-training programs seemed trivial. He wanted to make big changes. That would require a whole different level of power and influence. And no place could propel him to that level like Harvard Law School.

There, Obama thrived. In 1990, he made history as the first black president of the *Harvard Law Review.*

Upon graduation, he could have worked for any law firm in the country. But he had another plan. This took him back to Chicago and into politics.

In 1996, he ran for the state senate. The problem was that his opponent, Alice Palmer, had much more political clout than he did. He couldn't beat her in a straight-up fight. He had to find another way to win. Probing her filing documents, he found enough questionable signatures to challenge her candidacy. Palmer was disqualified, and the seat was his.

In 2004, he ran for the US Senate. It figured to be a close race, but Obama again got "lucky." The *Chicago Tribune* published his Republican opponent's sealed divorce records, which included salacious accusations that he had asked his wife to accompany him to sex clubs. The contest, at that point, was over.

Obama coasted to an easy win—so easy that the Democratic Party gave him a prime slot at that year's national convention. In a speech that rocked the delegates, he declared, "There's not a black America and a white America . . . there's the United States of America."

This was a message to build a presidential campaign on. That campaign wouldn't be long in coming.

Obama's restlessness quickly manifested itself in the Senate. Being a member of that exclusive club bored him. Getting things done took forever.

After only two years, Obama made it clear he was going for the top job: the presidency in 2008. His biggest competition was no less than former First Lady and New York Senator Hillary Clinton. She could match him with historic "firsts": if Obama could be the first black president, Hillary could be the first female president.

They battled it out for five months, but the result was never really in doubt. Obama was just too fresh, too charismatic, too exciting, and too chosen. His support from young people was overwhelming. They flocked to his message of "hope and change." In the end, Hillary seemed like old news. So did the Republican nominee, Arizona Senator and Vietnam War hero John McCain.

Obama ran away with the popular vote, 53 percent to 46 percent, and the Electoral College, 365 to 173.

But did Americans know the man they had just elected? Aside from the catchy slogans and the soaring rhetoric, what did Obama really believe? The answer for the few who chose to look deeper is found in a speech he gave in Columbia, Missouri, on the eve of the election. "We are five days away from fundamentally transforming the United States of America."

He was right!

Born into abject poverty in rural Virginia, Carol Swain earned five degrees and obtained early tenure at Princeton and full professorship at Vanderbilt, where she was professor of political science and a professor of law. Today she is a sought-after cable news contributor, prominent national speaker, and bestselling author.

In addition to three presidential appointments, Swain is a former Distinguished Senior Fellow for Constitutional Studies with the Texas Public Policy Foundation, having also served on the Tennessee Advisory Committee to the US Civil Rights Commission, the National Endowment for the Humanities, and the 1776 Commission.

An award-winning political scientist, cited three times by the US Supreme Court, she has authored or edited eleven published books and numerous opinion pieces for major national publications. Her television appearances include BBC Radio and TV, C-SPAN, ABC News, CNN, and FOX News.

CHAPTER 55

BARACK OBAMA

Transforming America

By Carol Swain

Shortly before Barack Obama was elected the forty-fourth president of the United States, he told an enthusiastic crowd of supporters that he wanted to "fundamentally" transform America.

Over the next eight years, America found out what he meant.

Three issues epitomized the transformation Obama had in mind.

1. *Race relations*

2. *Healthcare*

3. *And foreign policy*

Let's take each one in turn.

Race Relations

Could it be that when Obama said he wanted to fundamentally transform America, he was talking about a post-racial society where skin color didn't matter? Indeed, as a biracial American, half white, half black, he seemed the perfect figure to make this a reality.

But it was not to be. Instead, Obama's actions fueled racial division in America.

In July 2009, when a white police officer briefly arrested a black Harvard professor as a suspected burglar, Obama accused the police officer, a man with no history of bigotry, of racism.

In July 2013, after a Hispanic volunteer security guard was acquitted of the murder of a young black man in Florida, Obama attributed the verdict to racism.

And then, in August 2014, when a black teenager who had just robbed a convenience store was shot by a white police officer in Ferguson, Missouri, Obama again charged racism. His own Justice Department later acquitted the officer of racial animus.

Whereas in the decade leading up to Obama's presidency, racial tensions had sharply declined, they were now inflamed by the man who so many Americans hoped would extinguish them.

Healthcare

Where Bill Clinton had failed, Barack Obama would succeed.

He would bring the United States closer to the "enlightened" nations of Europe, all of which had socialized their healthcare systems.

Obama marshaled his rhetorical skills to achieve this goal. If he had to engage in outright falsehoods to get what he wanted, that was okay. "If you like your doctor, you can keep your doctor" was one of his constant refrains. But it wasn't true. Neither was his assertion that the program would save Americans thousands of dollars in healthcare costs.

Despite his best efforts, Obama couldn't sell his plan to a majority of the American people. It turned out that most of them liked the healthcare coverage they had.

On Christmas Eve 2009, in the middle of the night, the Democrats rammed the twenty-five-hundred-page Affordable Care Act through the Senate. Asked what was in the legislation, House Speaker Nancy Pelosi famously responded, "We have to pass the bill so that you can find out what is in it. . . ."

Within a few years, twenty-five hundred pages turned into eleven thousand pages of new regulations, healthcare costs ballooned, and many people were forced to give up the doctor they trusted. But for Obama, it was all worth it: he had transformed the nation's healthcare system.

Foreign Policy

Since the Iranian Revolution in 1979, American presidents have viewed Iran as a dangerous enemy. Obama believed he could transform this adversarial relationship.

The centerpiece of Obama's new policy would be the Joint Comprehensive Plan of Action, popularly known as the Iran Nuclear Deal. The key feature of the plan was to limit Iran's ability to make a nuclear weapon for fifteen years. In exchange, Obama would lift sanctions and release $150 billion of Iranian assets frozen in US banks.

The deal deeply unsettled many Americans, including some Democrats, and especially Israel and its supporters. First, a short-term infusion of billions of dollars—almost certainly to be used to fund Israel's enemies Hamas and Hezbollah—posed immediate danger. Second, a nuclear-armed Iran—even fifteen years in the future—threatened the existence of Israel.

When Israel's leaders strongly objected to the agreement, Obama ignored them.

Knowing he couldn't get a treaty through the Senate, Obama issued an executive order to carry out his plan. A giant military plane soon landed in Tehran with $400 million in cash.

The Iran nuclear deal turned US foreign policy on its head. America would now trust Iran to behave like a good global citizen, ignoring opposition from US allies, Israel and Saudi Arabia.

No matter. Obama knew best.

But when he left office in 2017, the region, as many had predicted, was in chaos. Syria was wracked by civil war. Iraq was essentially an Iranian puppet government. And Hamas and Hezbollah were stronger than ever.

Race relations.

Healthcare.

Foreign policy.

Obama had, indeed, achieved his goal. He had fundamentally transformed America. But he had done more than that. He had fundamentally transformed the world.

⁘

Born into abject poverty in rural Virginia, Carol Swain earned five degrees and obtained early tenure at Princeton and full professorship at Vanderbilt where she was professor of political science and a professor of law. Today she is a sought-after cable news contributor, prominent national speaker, and bestselling author.

In addition to three presidential appointments, Swain is a former Distinguished Senior Fellow for Constitutional Studies with the Texas Public Policy Foundation, having also served on the Tennessee Advisory Committee to the US Civil Rights Commission, the National Endowment for the Humanities, and the 1776 Commission.

An award-winning political scientist, cited three times by the US Supreme Court, she has authored or edited eleven published books and numerous opinion pieces for major national publications. Her television appearances include BBC Radio and TV, C-SPAN, ABC News, CNN, and FOX News.

CHAPTER 56

DONALD TRUMP

The MAGA President

By Niall Ferguson

One day in the future, historians will be struck by the contrast between two contemporary narratives of the Trump era.

According to one narrative, the forty-fifth and forty-seventh president of the United States, Donald J. Trump, was a modern-day Caesar—an autocrat who, by ignoring constitutional constraints, aspired to end the American republic.

According to the other narrative, this same man was a courageous tribune of the people who, by taking on corrupt and predatory elites, saved the republic.

Which version is right?

Let's find out.

Donald Trump was born on June 14, 1946, in Queens, New York, the son of a successful real estate developer.

After graduating from the Wharton School, Trump joined the family firm. A high-stakes risk-taker, Trump's towers, casinos, and resorts generated remarkable quantities of cash, debt, and litigation, not to mention publicity.

In 2004, the risk-taker gambled on a second career—as the host of the "reality" TV show *The Apprentice*. It made Trump a star.

But it was his third career as a politician that ultimately made Trump the most famous person in the world.

On June 16, 2015, Trump announced that he was seeking the Republican nomination for the presidency. Few people took him seriously. He had dabbled in politics before but had never run for any political office.

Yet Trump struck a chord with his attacks on illegal immigration from Mexico and unfair trade with China. His unvarnished, unscripted style inspired a new populist political movement with the slogan "Make

America Great Again"—MAGA. While the coastal elites had benefited from globalization, many Americans felt left behind. In this brash billionaire, with his viral tweets, they found a champion.

The pundits and pollsters forecast victory for the Democratic candidate, Hillary Clinton.

They were wrong.

True, Clinton won the popular vote, but Trump won the vote that mattered, the Electoral College: 304 to 227.

A fractious coalition between his campaign team, the Republican establishment, and a succession of generals and businessmen, Trump's first administration often seemed chaotic. But in terms of Trump's core objectives, it was highly successful.

On the campaign trail, he had promised to build a "big, beautiful wall" on the nation's southern border. He succeeded metaphorically. In 2017, in just his first year as president, apprehensions at the US-Mexico border dropped to a forty-six-year low.

Thanks to Trump's tax cuts and deregulation, real median household income rose significantly for the first time since 1999—by 10 percent between 2016 and 2019.

When Trump took office, the Islamic State terrorist organization had overrun large parts of Syria and Iraq. Within two years, it was effectively wiped out.

The Abraham Accords that Trump negotiated represented a geopolitical breakthrough in relations between Israel and the Arab countries.

And by imposing tariffs, Trump pressured China into a trade deal that began to address the economic imbalances between the two countries.

Yet to his opponents, Trump was a would-be dictator. The Democrats even claimed he was a pawn of Russian President Vladimir Putin. When that charge could not be substantiated, the Democrats impeached Trump on the ground that he had pressured Ukrainian president Volodymyr Zelensky to investigate former Vice President Joe Biden. The Senate acquitted Trump.

It took a highly contagious virus originating from Wuhan, China, to succeed where Trump's political opponents had failed.

The COVID-19 pandemic threw the Western world into a panic. America, like most countries, locked down. This expedient did not reduce mortality by much, but it did plunge the economy into a deep crisis.

An incident in Minneapolis, Minnesota, in May 2020 further ripped the social fabric. During a routine arrest, a black suspect named George Floyd, a petty criminal and drug user, died while being restrained by a white police officer, Derek Chauvin. Subsequently, Chauvin was convicted of unintentional second-degree murder.

Orchestrated by the group Black Lives Matter, and fanned by Democrats and the media, protests and riots erupted across the country. It was in this feverish atmosphere that the 2020 election campaign took place.

The Democrats insisted on mail-in balloting, ostensibly to avoid spreading the virus. In many states, they got their way; unwisely, Trump discouraged Republicans from casting postal votes. Despite spending most of the race in the basement of his Delaware home, the Democratic candidate, Joe Biden, won 81 million votes, 15 million more than Barack Obama had in 2012, to Trump's 74 million.

Trump was convinced the election had been stolen. On January 6, 2021, he encouraged a large crowd to march to the Capitol. Partly because of woefully inadequate policing, the protest ran out of control. In the aftermath, the Democrats again impeached Trump. When this failed, they unleashed a barrage of criminal and civil cases against him.

But what didn't kill him made him stronger, figuratively and literally. Trump ran for reelection. Not only did he beat his Republican challengers and withstand a guilty verdict, he survived two assassination attempts.

In November 2024, Trump defeated Vice President Kamala Harris in the greatest comeback in American political history, this time winning the popular vote as well as the Electoral College.

The final historical verdict on Donald Trump, the ultimate American risk-taker, cannot yet be returned. Caesar or savior?

Sir Niall Ferguson is the Milbank Family Senior Fellow at the Hoover Institution, Stanford University, and a Senior Faculty Fellow of the Belfer Center for Science and International Affairs at Harvard, where he served for twelve years as the Laurence A. Tisch Professor of History. He is the author of sixteen books.

In 2003, Ferguson wrote and presented a six-part history of the British Empire for Channel 4, the UK broadcaster. The accompanying book, *Empire: The Rise and Demise of the British World Order and the Lessons for Global Power*, was a bestseller in both Britain and the United States. The sequel, *Colossus: The Rise and Fall of the American Empire*, was published in 2004 by Penguin, and prompted *Time* magazine to name him one of the one hundred most influential people in the world. The international bestseller, *The Ascent of Money: A Financial History of the World*, followed in 2008; it was a PBS series, winning the International Emmy award for Best Documentary, as well as the Handelszeitung Economics Book Prize.

An accomplished biographer, Ferguson published *High Financier: The Lives and Time of Siegmund Warburg* in 2010 and is currently writing a life of Henry Kissinger, the first volume of which was published in 2015—to critical acclaim—as *Kissinger, 1923–1968: The Idealist*. The book won the 2016 Council on Foreign Relations Arthur Ross Book Award. Other notable books include *Civilization: The West and the Rest* (2011), *The Square and the Tower* (2018), and *Doom: The Politics of Catastrophe* (2021).

Niall Ferguson is married to the author and women's rights activist Ayaan Hirsi Ali.

CHAPTER 57

JOE BIDEN

Decline and Fall

By Tevi Troy

Joe Biden was a young man in a hurry. Elected to the US Senate at the age of twenty-nine, he spent four decades dreaming of becoming president. But then, in one of American history's tragic ironies, when he finally got there, he was incapable of doing the job. Father Time had exacted a cruel price.

Joseph Robinette—forever known as Joe—Biden was born in the coal-mining town of Scranton, Pennsylvania, on November 20, 1942. His father moved the family to Wilmington, Delaware, when Biden was ten, but Biden would always stress his working-class Scranton origins.

Young Joe was popular and a good athlete, but just got by academically. At Syracuse Law School, he graduated seventy-sixth out of a class of eighty-five.

After getting caught plagiarizing a law review article, a pattern emerged that persisted throughout his life: if he didn't like a version of his past, he'd make up a better one. Examples include getting arrested when trying to visit South African civil rights activist Nelson Mandela in prison, being shot at while touring Iraq as a senator, and his uncle getting eaten by cannibals in Papua New Guinea during World War II—all fabrications.

In 1972, after a brief tenure on a Delaware county council, he challenged incumbent Republican Senator J. Caleb Boggs. Biden's youthful energy captured the voters' imagination. In a shocking upset, he defeated Boggs by three thousand votes.

Before he could take office, tragedy struck. In December 1972, his wife, Neilia, and one-year-old daughter, Amy, were killed in a car crash. His sons, Beau and Hunter, were badly injured.

Biden pushed past his grief and entered the Senate, the youngest member in that exclusive club.

There, Biden thrived. There's no doubt that he had political skills. You don't get elected to the Senate seven times, vice president twice, and ultimately president without being good at politics. Winning reelection after reelection, he advanced in seniority and influence.

But make no mistake, the presidency was always his goal.

In 1987, he ran for the Democratic nomination. That attempt failed when he was caught plagiarizing a speech by a British politician. He ran again in 2007 but got swept away by Barack Obama.

Then Obama, to the surprise of many, tapped Biden to be his running mate. It seemed like a good match of young gun and old pro.

As vice president, Biden served loyally for eight years, but when it came time for Obama to bless a successor, he opted for his former Secretary of State Hillary Clinton. It was a bitter pill.

When Donald Trump shocked the world by defeating Clinton in 2016, Biden's presidential embers stirred again. At age seventy-seven, he reached for the brass ring one more time.

In a close election, Biden came out on top, realizing his life's ambition.

But he had come to the highest office, not at the apex of his powers, but in his old age. Once a smooth-talking pol, he now struggled to string together complete sentences.

Biden's old age might have been forgiven if, as promised, he'd unified the nation by governing as a sensible moderate. Instead, he further divided it by moving far to the left.

For example, he changed Title IX to include gender, allowing men to compete in women's sports. He mandated that the federal government favor "diversity, equity, and inclusion" over merit. He equated people who disagreed with him on racial issues with white supremacists. And he signed the Inflation Reduction Act, which actually boosted inflation by flooding the economy with deficit dollars, almost all of it going to dubious green energy projects, like electric school buses.

Biden did little better on the foreign policy front. By precipitously withdrawing American troops from Afghanistan in the summer of 2021, he left that country in chaos and handed over billions of dollars' worth of military hardware to radical Islamists. He tried to mollify Iran by easing sanctions, providing them with billions in cash, much of which went to terrorist groups like Hamas and Hezbollah. He said he'd defend Israel after the barbaric Hamas attacks on October 7, 2023, and then he micromanaged Israel the whole way. And finally, and perhaps most egregiously, he opened America's southern border to a virtually unrestricted flow of millions of illegal immigrants.

Through all of this, his cognitive decline became more and more obvious to anyone with eyes to see.

Still, as the 2024 election approached, the mainstream media continued to make excuses for him. Cable news host Joe Scarborough shamelessly declared, "This version . . . is the best Biden ever."

A June debate with Donald Trump, once again the GOP nominee, exploded this obvious untruth. Fifty million Americans watched a president whose best days were behind him. The jig was up. Democrats, fearful of electoral disaster, now demanded Biden withdraw from the race.

After an unprecedented pressure campaign by leaders of his own party, Biden relented and endorsed his vice president, Kamala Harris.

With Biden gifting her the nomination, Harris went on to lose to Donald Trump. Then Biden further sullied his reputation with a host of unsavory pardons and executive actions on his way out the door.

Joe Biden had achieved his dream—the presidency—but the verdict of history is unlikely to be kind.

Tevi Troy is a presidential historian and bestselling author. His latest book is *Fight House: Rivalries in the White House from Truman to Trump*.

Troy has extensive White House experience, having served in positions including deputy assistant and then acting assistant to the president for domestic policy.

He is the author of *What Jefferson Read, Ike Watched, and Obama Tweeted*; *Intellectuals and the American Presidency*; and *Shall We Wake the President?* He has written over 250 articles for the *New York Times*, the *Wall Street Journal*, the *Washington Post*, and *National Review*. He has appeared on CNBC, CNN, C-SPAN, FOX News, FOX Business, and *NewsHour*, among other outlets.

Troy has a B.S. in industrial and labor relations from Cornell University and an M.A. and Ph.D. in American civilization from the University of Texas at Austin.

Conclusion

Well, was Warren Harding a better president than you thought he was?

Did you ever think of Chester Arthur as the ultimate party animal?

And who knew that Rutherford B. Hayes and Benjamin Harrison were so impressive?

Why is James Monroe always forgotten among the five founding presidents?

Is it impossible *not* to love Calvin Coolidge?

Do Washington and Franklin Roosevelt deserve their halos?

Do Hoover and Nixon deserve their horns?

Did Obama transform the country for the better or worse?

Will Trump take a place near the top or near the bottom of presidential rankings?

There are no "right" answers. Americans will always debate one another about their presidents' successes and failures. And that's a good thing because to have the debate at all means you know something about the players.

It's our hope that this book has equipped you with that basic knowledge.

It's also our hope that you'll continue your presidential education.

There's a reason why that's important. To have any chance of a shared future, we need to understand our shared past. We can be divided along political lines, but we should be broadly united along historical lines. Knowing something about the presidents will go a long way to making that a reality.

America has never been a perfect country—obviously. Our presidents are not perfect people—obviously. But after reading these short biographies, I think you'll agree that the country—across its 250-year history—has constantly struggled to better itself.

And invariably, it's been our presidents leading the way, usually forward but sometimes backward.

Now that you know something about all the presidents, have you learned anything about what makes a good president? That would be a useful question to answer as you contemplate your next vote.

Let us leave you with a final fun thought. If you have trouble falling asleep, instead of counting sheep, try counting presidents—in order. You'll probably never make it to Lincoln (number sixteen). And if you really want to knock yourself out, include the years they served in office. You can exclude poor William Henry Harrison. As you'll remember, he lasted only a month.

Hail to the Chiefs.

Acknowledgments

To my dear friend and cofounder, Dennis Prager, who has been closely involved with all our 5-Minute Videos since our inception, including this Presidents' Series. It's not called PragerU for nothing.

Allen Estrin, Editor

About PragerU

PragerU is a nonprofit educational media enterprise that serves audiences of all ages—students, parents, and anyone with an open mind eager to learn. Its materials—short videos, podcasts, books, and magazines—present ideas grounded in truth, guided by common sense, and informed by historical context.